Milan Bata Petrovic
School of rhythm guitar
GUITAR & SONG

Publisher
Milan Petrovic

For publisher
Milan Petrovic

Chief editor
Milan Petrovic

Reviewer
Prof Vera Ogrizovic

Editor
Prof Tomislav Pavlovic

Front page
Dijana Antanasijevic

Computer processing
Milan Bata Petrovic

ISMN 979-0-9014226-0-5

Milan Bata Petrovic

School of rhythm guitar

GUITAR & SONG

Edition

I dedicate the book to my sons,
Relja and David

I would like to express my appreciation to Vera Ogrizovic, prof. of guitar at Belgrade Music Academy, who showed a lot of understanding for my modest efforts in popularizing this beautiful instrument which I have always loved. Beside the professional reviews of my books, my special gratitude for the great moral support, and I am glad that this time we had the opportunity to cooperate in this capacity.

Contents

INTRODUCTION

For a long time I was thinking - how would a guitar book look like so it's learned with love, singing along, without theoretical consideration and with a minimum amount of necessary information. That's how I came to an idea, and, wrote this book, called *Guitar & Song*.
I would like for this book to be an inspiration to everyone searching for the secrets of this magical instrument and fall in love with a guitar as much as I have always been.

Notes:

- Given that the book is written in English, all the songs are in English language, except *Besame muco, La paloma* и *La Bamba*, which are in Spanish.

AUTHOR

Krusevac
12. 08. 2017.

I. GUITAR

A guitar is a popular musical instrument classified as a string instrument. The sound is projected either acoustically or through electrical amplification. The guitar is a type of chordophone, traditionally constructed from wood and strung with either gut, nylon or steel strings and distinguished from other chordophones by its construction and tuning. There are three main types of modern acoustic guitar: the classical guitar (nylon-string guitar), the steel-string acoustic guitar, and the archtop guitar. The tone of an acoustic guitar is produced by the strings's vibration, amplified by the body of the guitar, which acts as a resonating chamber.

Electric guitars, introduced in the 1930s, use an amplifier that can electronically manipulate and shape the tone.

The guitar is used in a wide variety of musical genres worldwide. It is recognized as a primary instrument in genres such as blues, bluegrass, country music, flamenco, folk, jazz, mariachi, metal, punk, reggae, rock, soul, and many forms of pop.

According to the type of music that is performed on the guitar (playing), it can be divided into:

1 / Classical Guitar
2 / Flamenco Guitar
3 / Popular solo guitar
4 / Rhythm Guitar
5 / Bass guitar

The subject of this book is the rhythm guitar.

Parts of the guitar

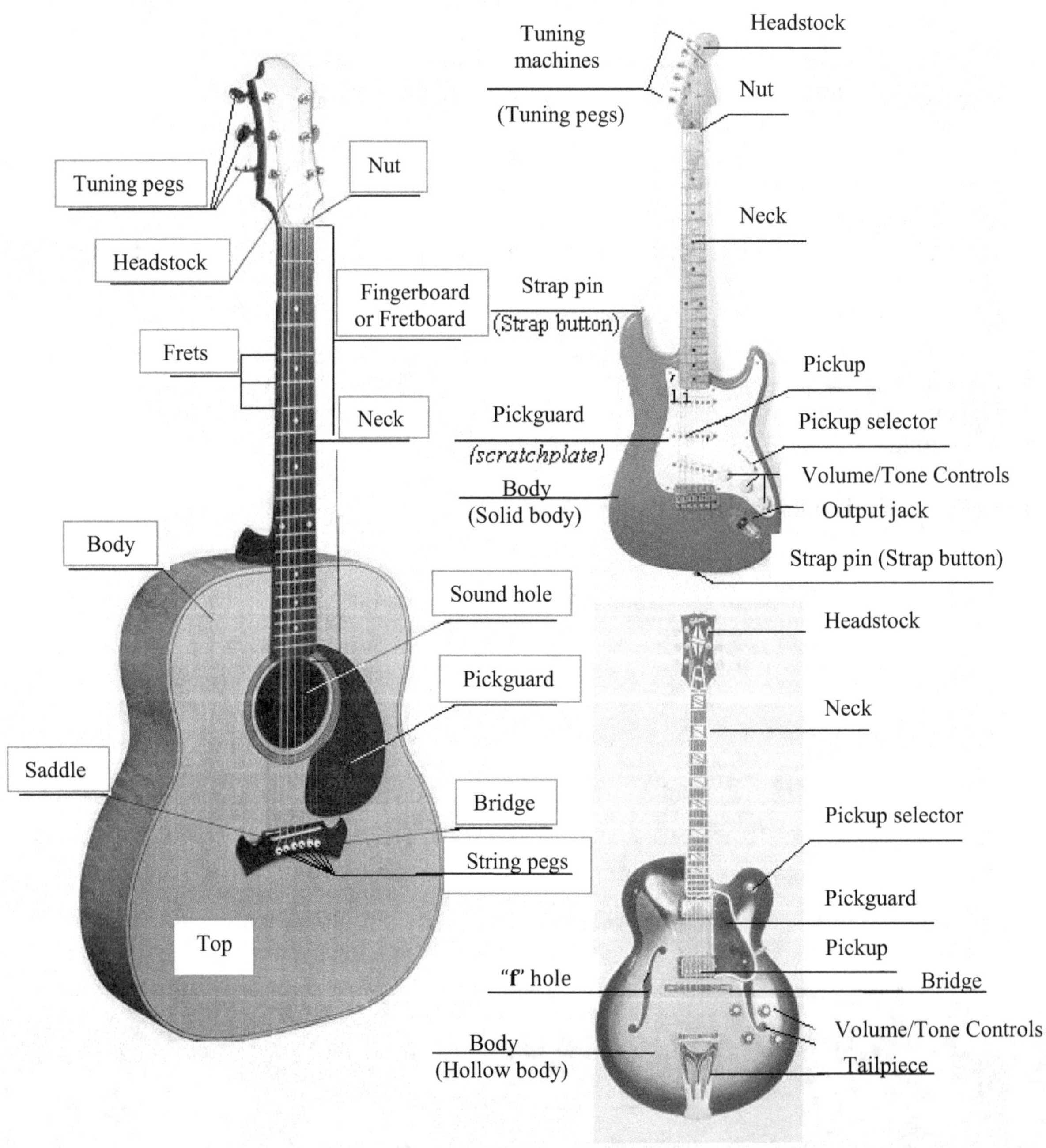

Tuning the Guitar

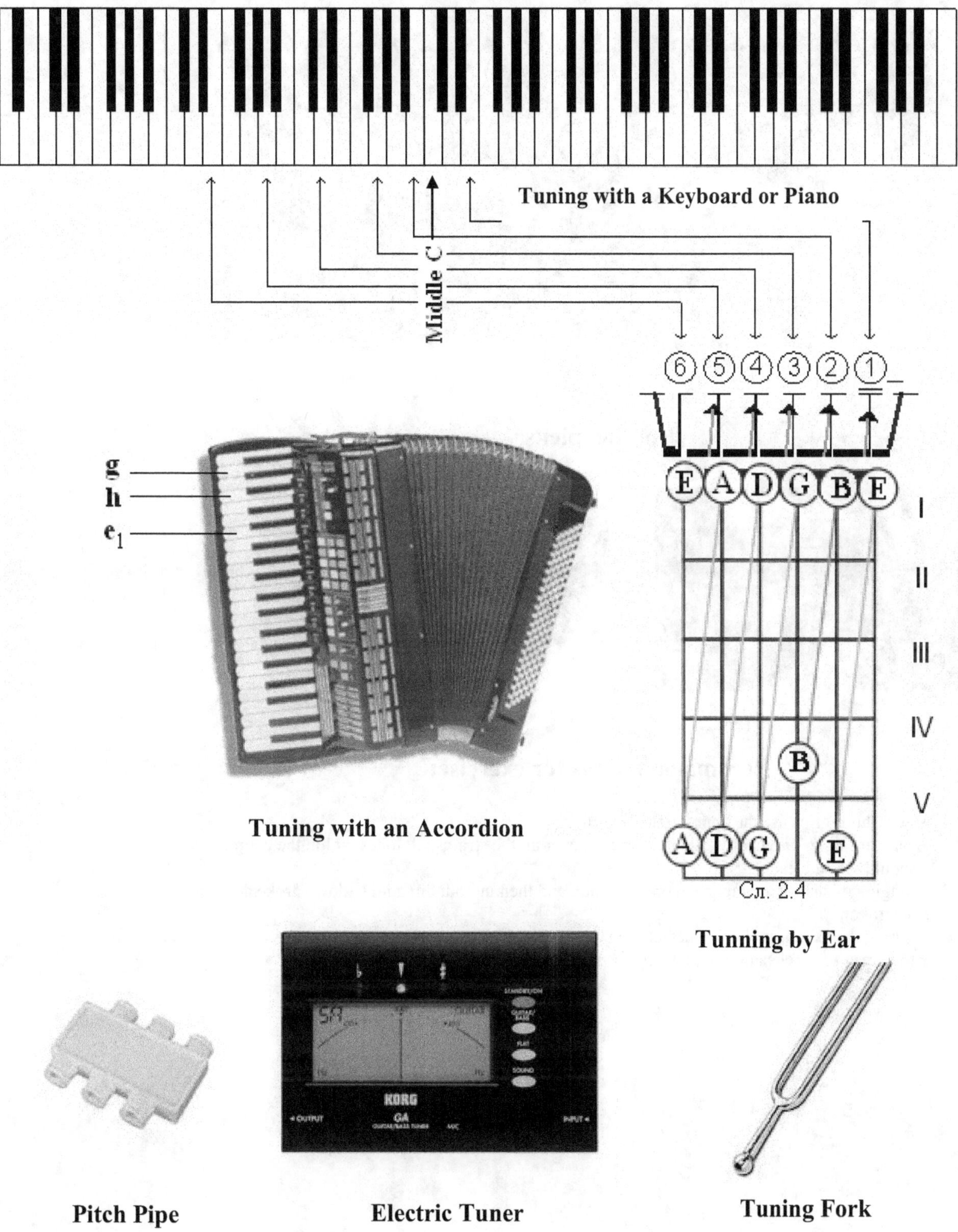

Tuning with an Accordion

Tunning by Ear

Pitch Pipe

Electric Tuner

Tuning Fork

Notes:
There are other, less well-known methods of tuning the guitar, as well as other types of guitar
tunings other than this (the Italian tuning);
Guitar can be tuned using the telephone. Signal on the phone with the handset emits a tone A.

Holding the guitar

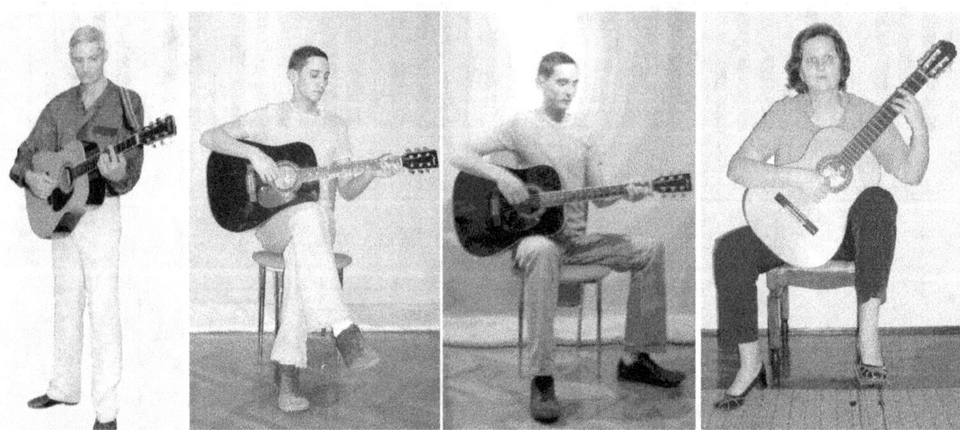

Holding picks

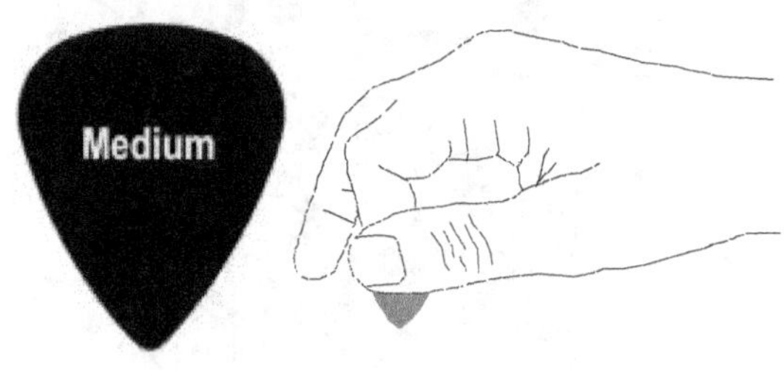

Recommendations for exercise:

- For Chord grips use the appropriate fingerings;
- for learning to grip chords, drag guitar pick over all the strings; all tones within the chords should sound clear;
- draging of strings to practice in one direction and then in both directions (downstroke and upstroke);
- during the exercises check whether the body is relaxed when playing;
- the greater the relaxation in playing when it is quieter.

II. CHORD AND CHORD GRIPS

Block diagrams of chords

These diagrams show how to play a chord. They include information about which frets are to be played by which fingers and which strings are to be played or not.

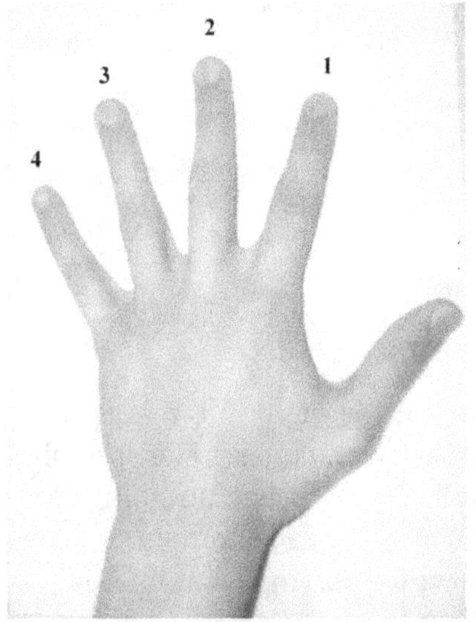

Tags for left hand fingerings

1 - first finger, index finger
2 - second finger, middle
3 - third finger, ring
4 - fourth finger, small

○ - An open circle means play the appropriate string open.

● - A filled circle means play the note on that particular fret and string.

✕ - An ✕ means mut or not play that string.

Blank Chord Diagram

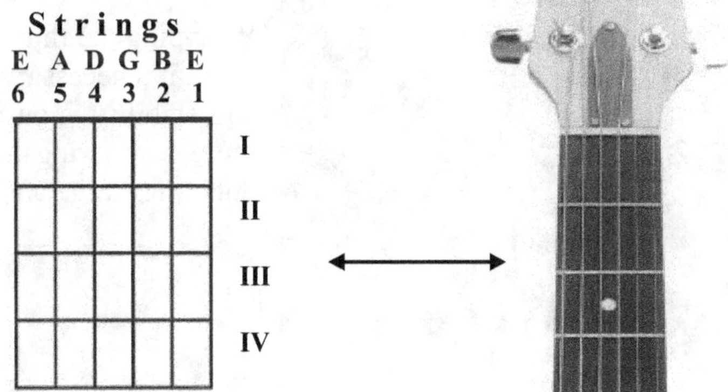

Example

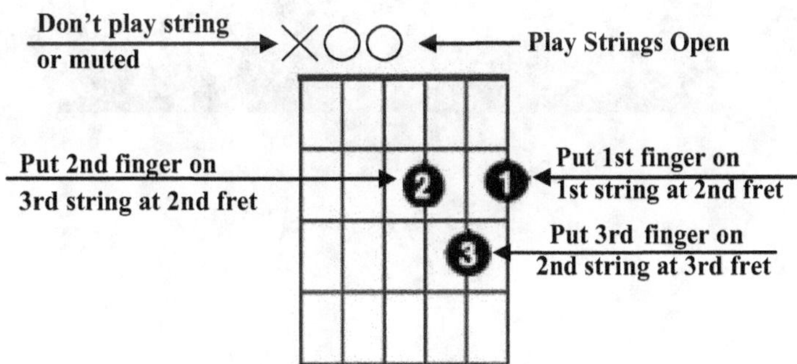

Chord diagram

Thumb Placement

Few things have as much direct impact on your playing as thumb placement! First of all, the thumb cannot and should not sit in one spot while you play.
There are three places where your thumb should be:

1 – At the "default" position
2 – Wedged behind the neck
3 – Wrapped over the fretboard

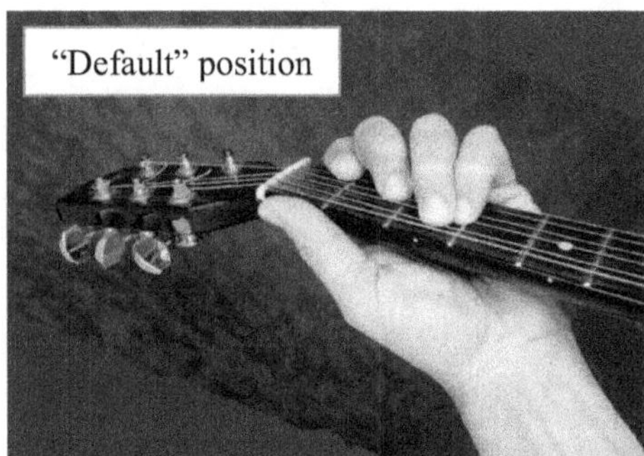

Just below the edge of the fretboard - it is the default position is for general use.

Contrary to what the classical teachers tell you, this is not the best thumb position for all techniques. This thumb position is problematic as well, since he has no ability to mute the 6th string (a requirement for clean chording).
This thumb placement is the best for playing barre chords[1].

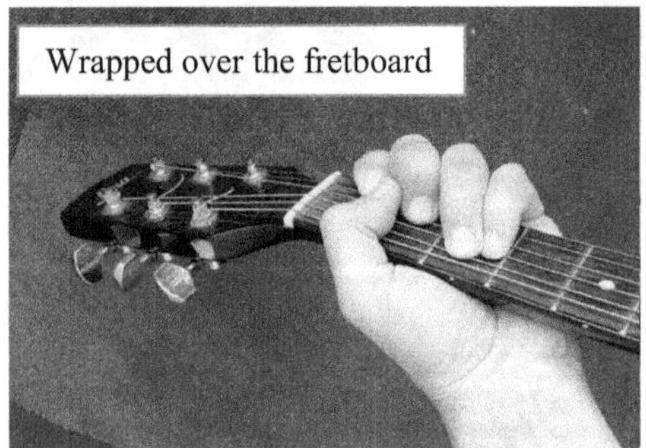

Wrapping the thumb[2] over the edge of the neck is used only when it's necessary! The wrapped thumb gives you leverage and stability. You also need to wrap the thumb in order to mute low strings, where the thumb actually does double duty – leverage and muting.

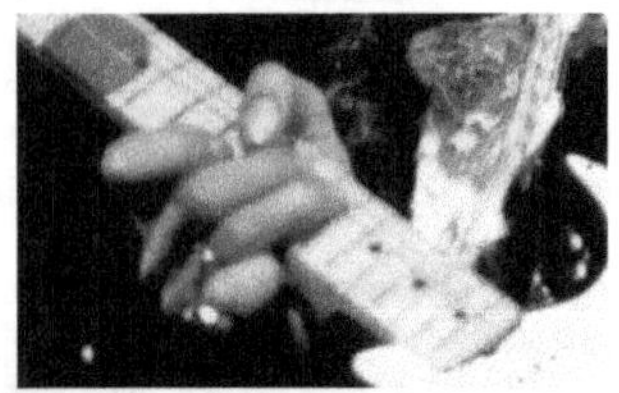

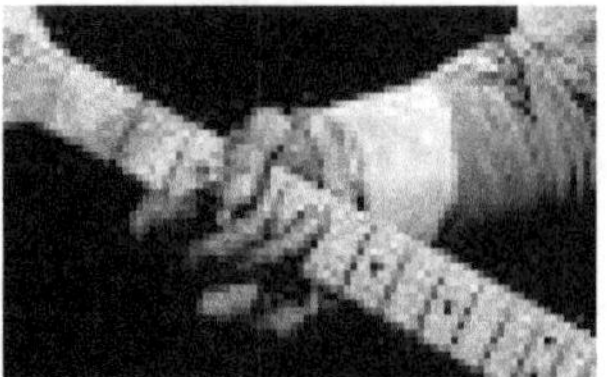

---

[1] See *Barre chords*, page 43.
[2] Jimi Hendrix used to wrap his thumb all the time instead of playing barres (see fig. 4).

Tags for the chords in this book

major - capital letter, for example, from **Cmajor** only **C**.
minor - capital letter and labeled m, for example, from **Cminor** only **Cm**;

Chord increased the basic tone for the semi tone - for example tons **D**, means **Dis**, is labeled $D^{\#}$.

Chord decreased the basic tone for the semi tone - for example tons **D**, means **Des**, is labeled D^{b}.

Dominant Seventh chord marks with a capital letter and a number seven, for example **C7**.
The other chords are also marked with a capital letter and characteristic mark that correspond, for example **C9, Cmaj7, Cdim,** ... etc.

Classification chords

The following classification shows chords[3] and chord grips in the order in which they are presented in the book.

Note:
The term of guitar chords usually applies also to the grip for the same chord.

Of guitar chord ussualy apples also to the grip for the same chord.

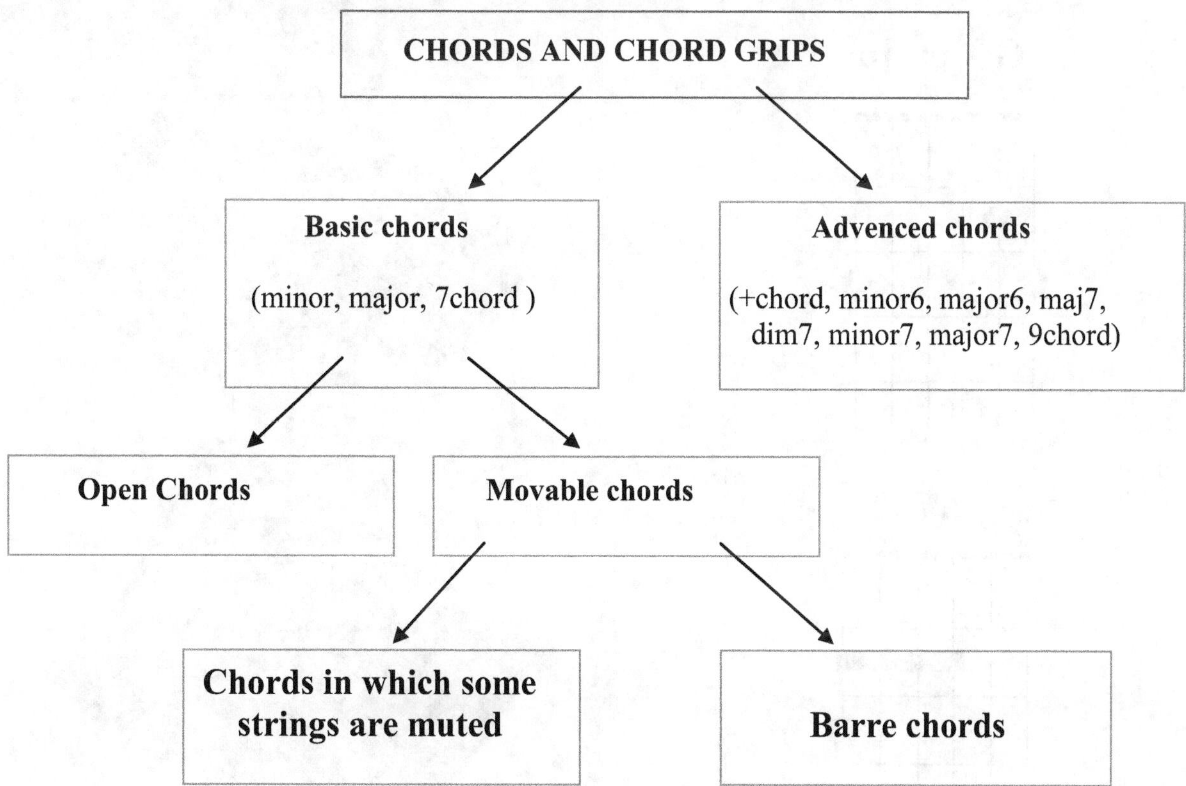

---

[3] The division on basic and advanced chords is internal, and is used only in this book. The same applies to the chords that are the subject of their study.

BASIC CHORDS
OPEN CHORDS

This term, open chords[4], refers to the chords that must be played in one position on the fingerboard, since one or more open strings are part of a chord.
Open chords are the easiest to play on guitar[5]. Learning open chords is important because it lays the foundation for learning how to form other chords.

Major chords and Dominant 7th chords

Combinacion D - major, G - major, A7

D - major

G - major

A7

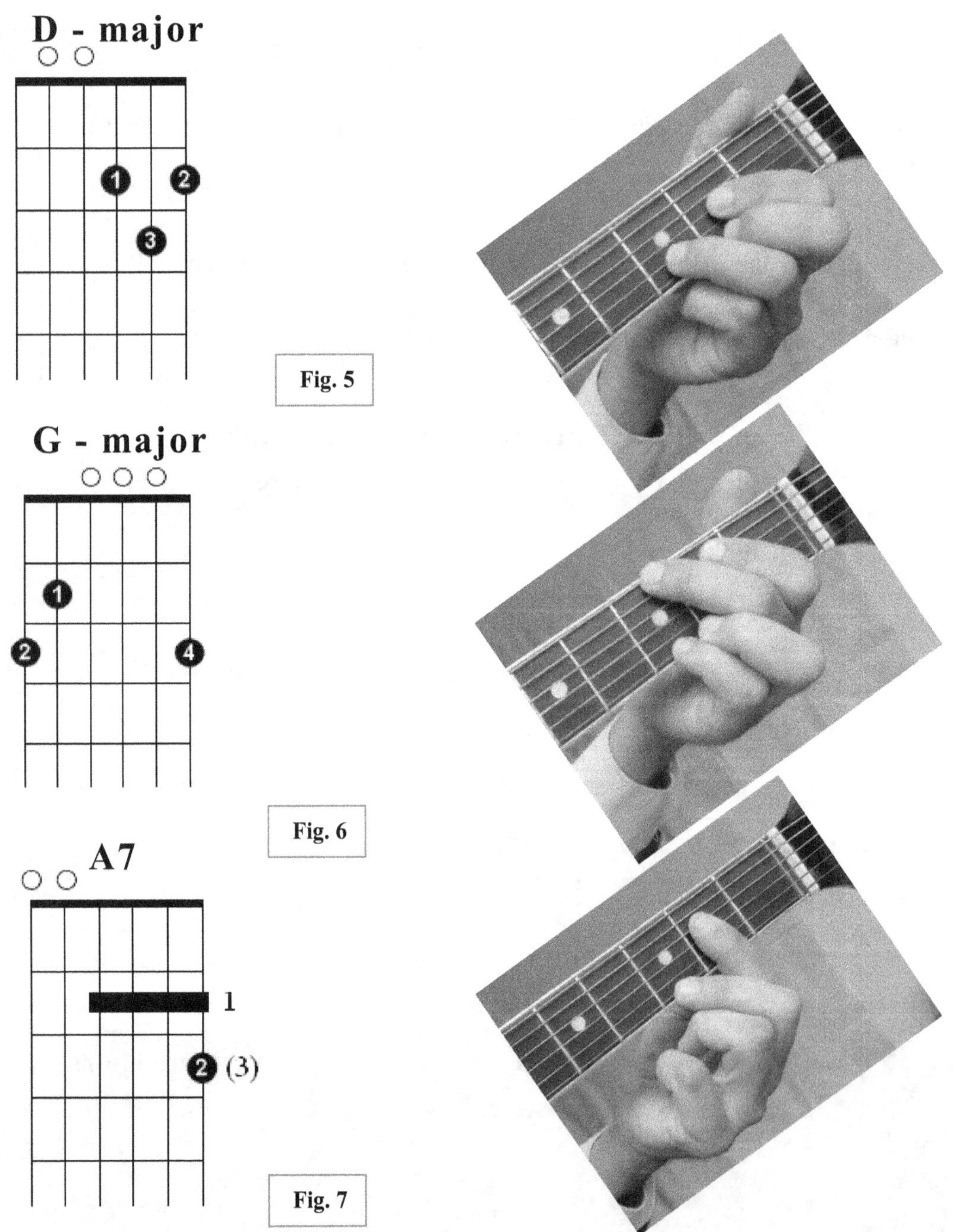

Fig. 5

Fig. 6

Fig. 7

---

[4] In music theory open chord has a different meaning in relation to the meaning of this title.
[5] Open chords are rarely used in professional playing rhythm guitar. However, they are used for guitar accompaniment for soft, lyrical poems; then there is a great expression of their use.

Example 1:

Oh, when the saints

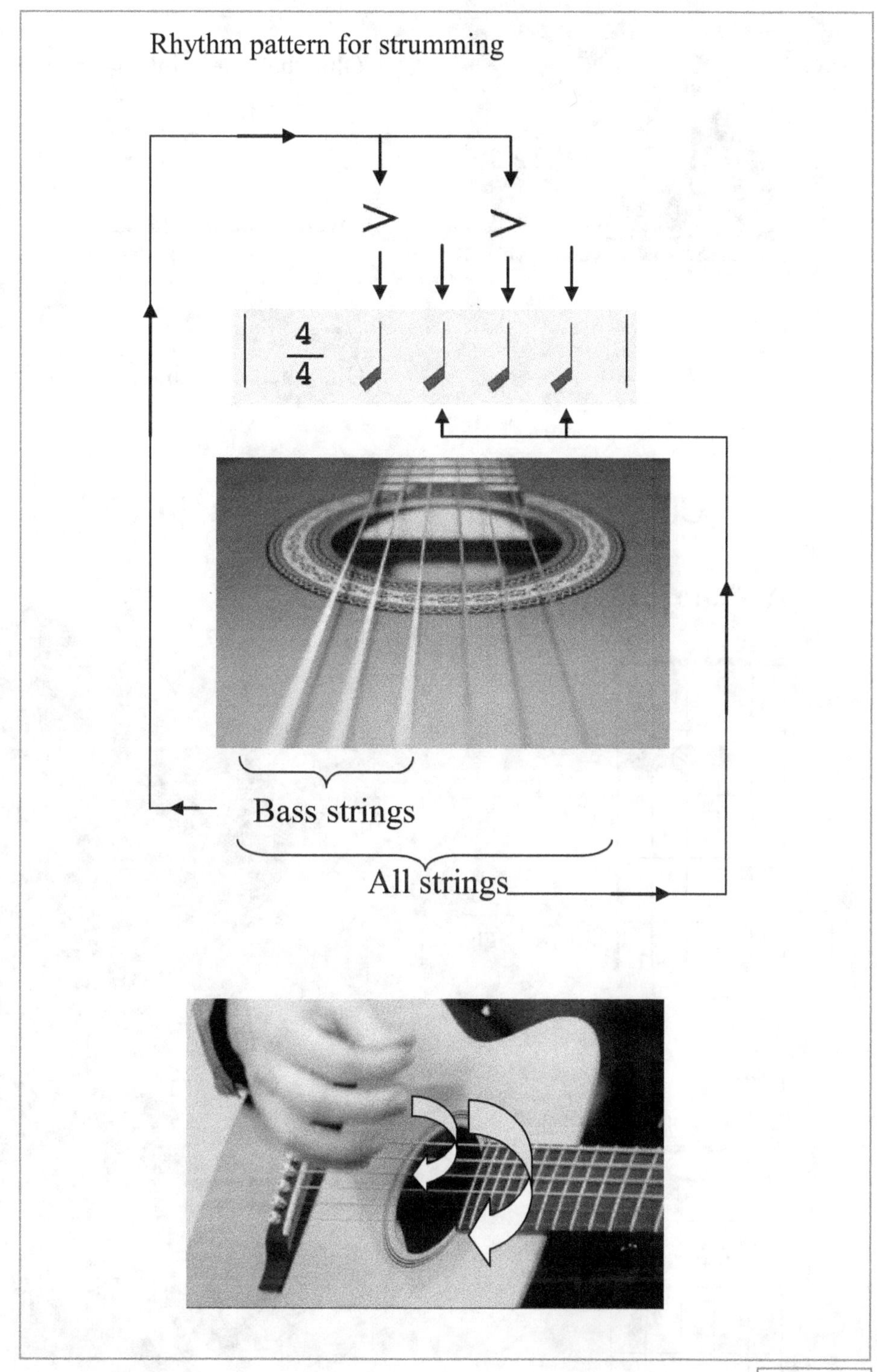

Note: -   Accented tone

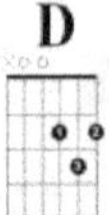

Oh, when the saints, go marcin in,

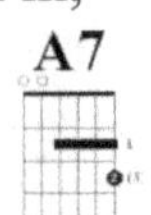

Oh, when the saints, go marcin in,

J want to be in that number,

Oh, when the saints, go marcin in.

Combination A - major, D - major, E7

A - major

Fig. 9

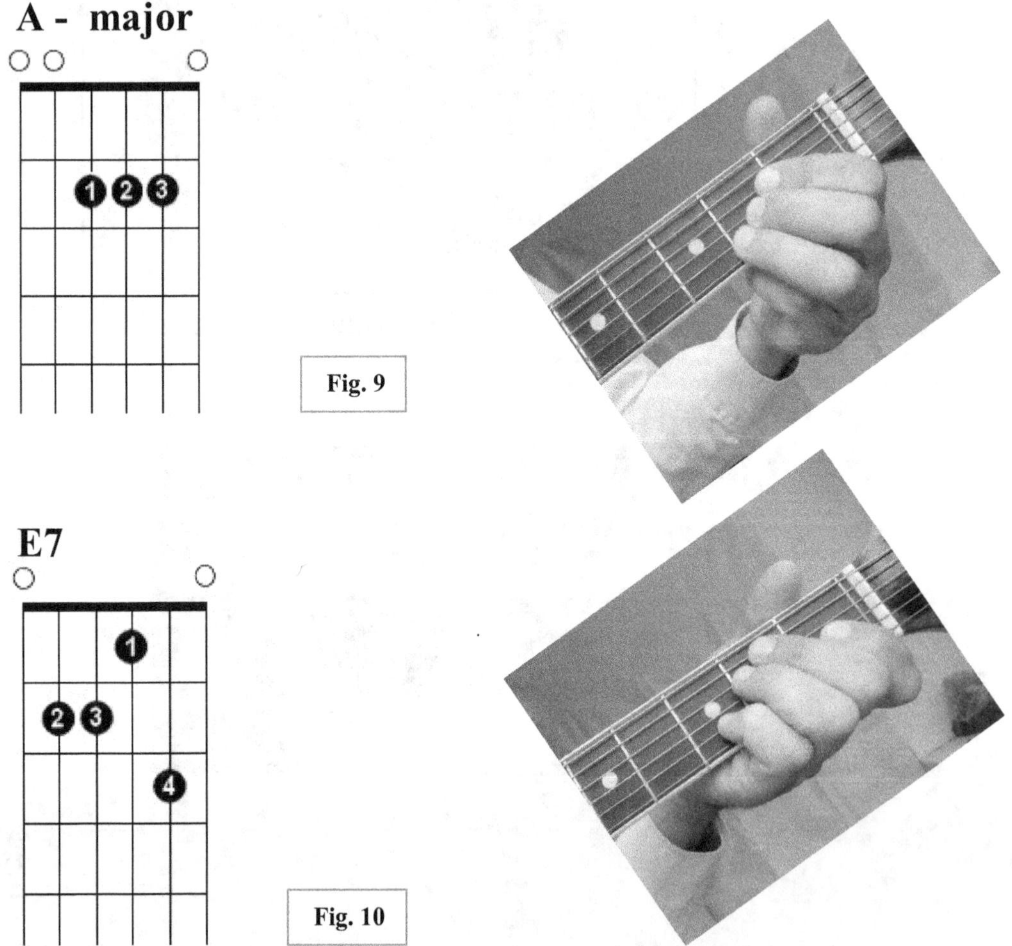

E7

Fig. 10

Note:
-   Chord Grip **D-major** is known (see fig. 5).

Example 2:   **Oh, Susanna**

Use the strumming as shown in fig. 8.

I come from Alabama with a banjo on my knee,

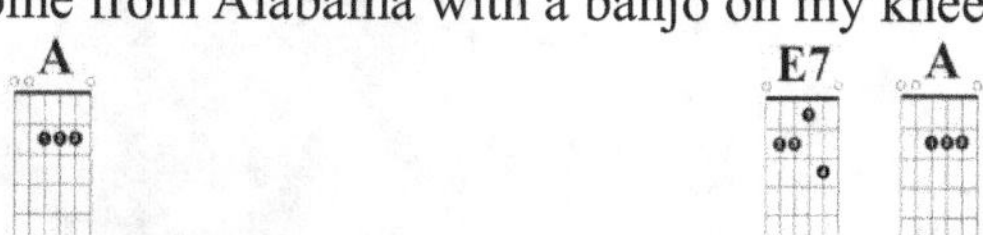

I'm going to Louisiana, my true love for to see

It rained all night the day I left, the weather it was dry,
The sun so hot I froze to death; Susanna, don't you cry.

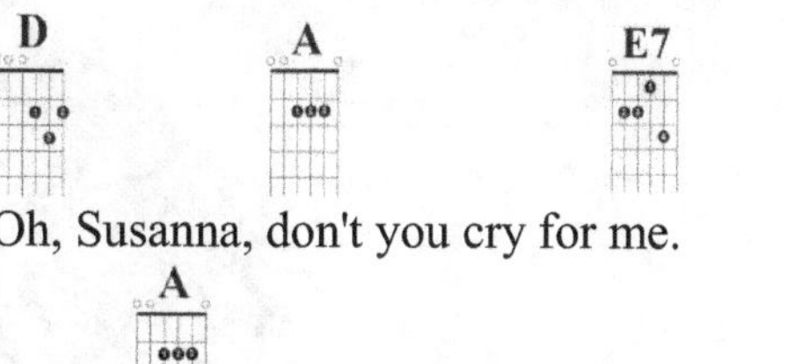

Oh, Susanna, don't you cry for me.

I come from Alabama with a banjo on my knee,

It rained all night the day I left, the weather it was dry,
The sun so hot I froze to death; Susanna, don't you cry.

Oh, Susanna …

Combination E - major, A - major, B7

E - major

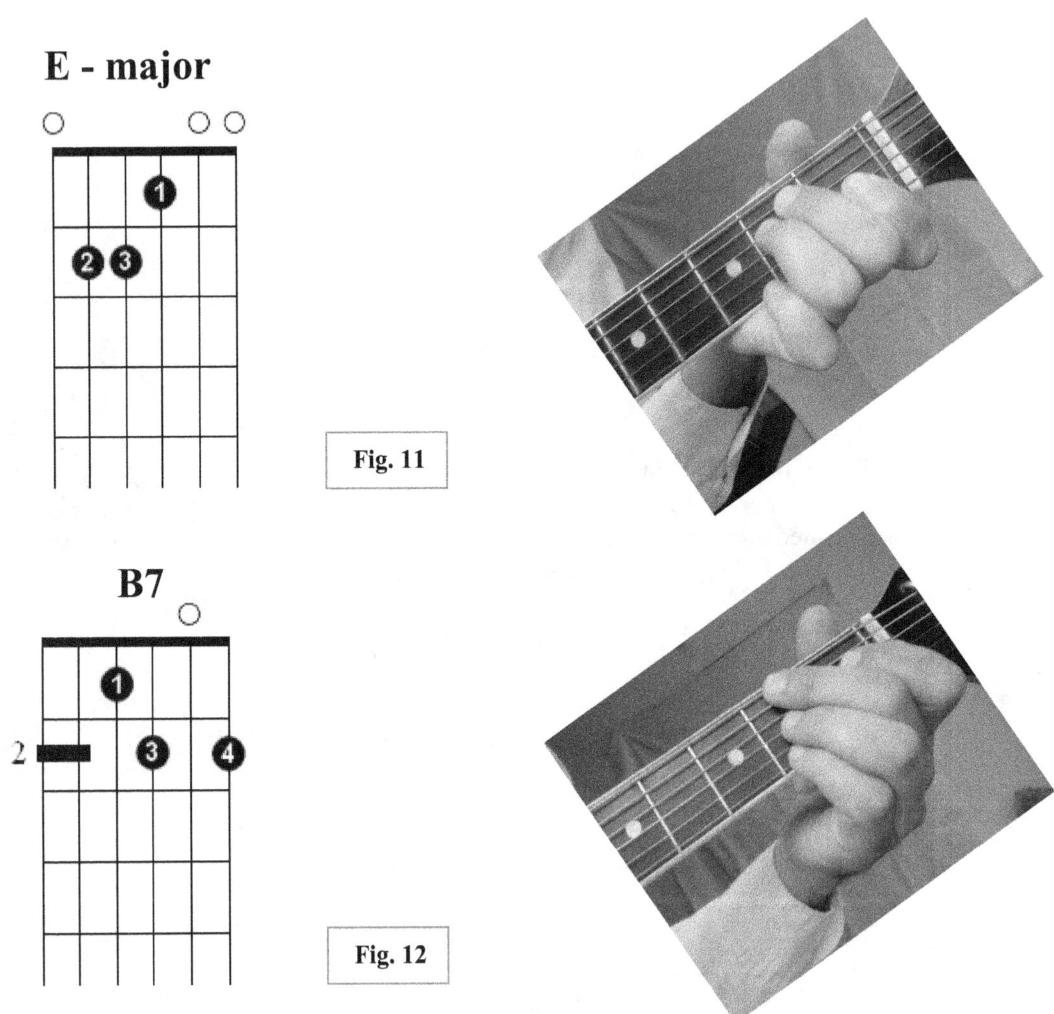

Fig. 11

B7

Fig. 12

Note:
- Chord Grip **A- major** is known (see fig. 9).

Example 3: **Banana boat**

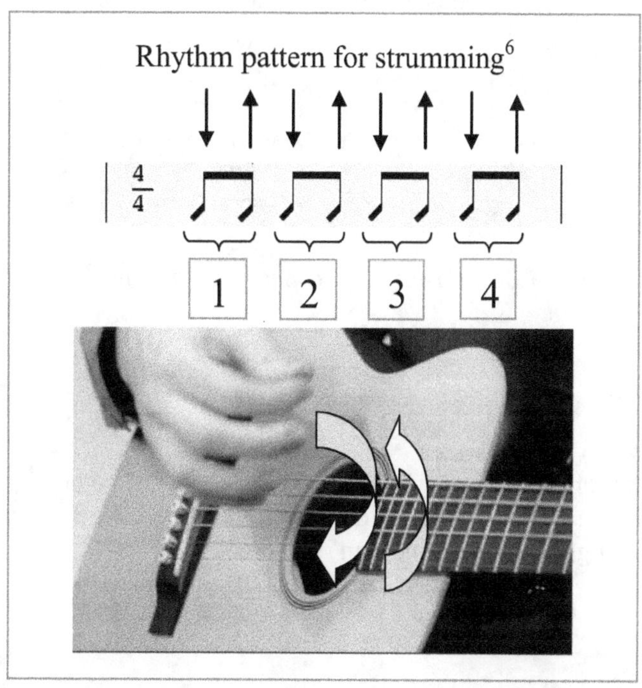

Fig. 13

E   B7   E

Day-oh Day-oh, Daylight come and me wann' go home

E   B7   E

Day, me say day, me say day, me say day, me say day, me say day,

E   B7   E

Daylight come and me wan' go home.

E

Six foot , seven foot, eight foot bunch

E   B7   E

Daylight come and me wan' go home

E

Six foot , seven foot, eight foot bunch.

E   B7   E

Daylight come and me wan' go home.

---

[6] This Strum is very offten in use. It can be applied to more musical genres. Right rhythm for the song *Banana Boat* is calypso (see page 58).

E   **B7**   **E**

Come mister tally man, tally me banana

E   **B7**

Daylight come and me wan' go home

E   **B7**

Come mister tally man tally me banana

E   **B7**

Daylight come and me wan' go home.

Day-oh Day-oh, Daylight come and me wann' go home,
Day, me say day, me say day, me say day, me say day, me say day,
Daylight come and me wan' go home.

Example 4:   **La paloma**

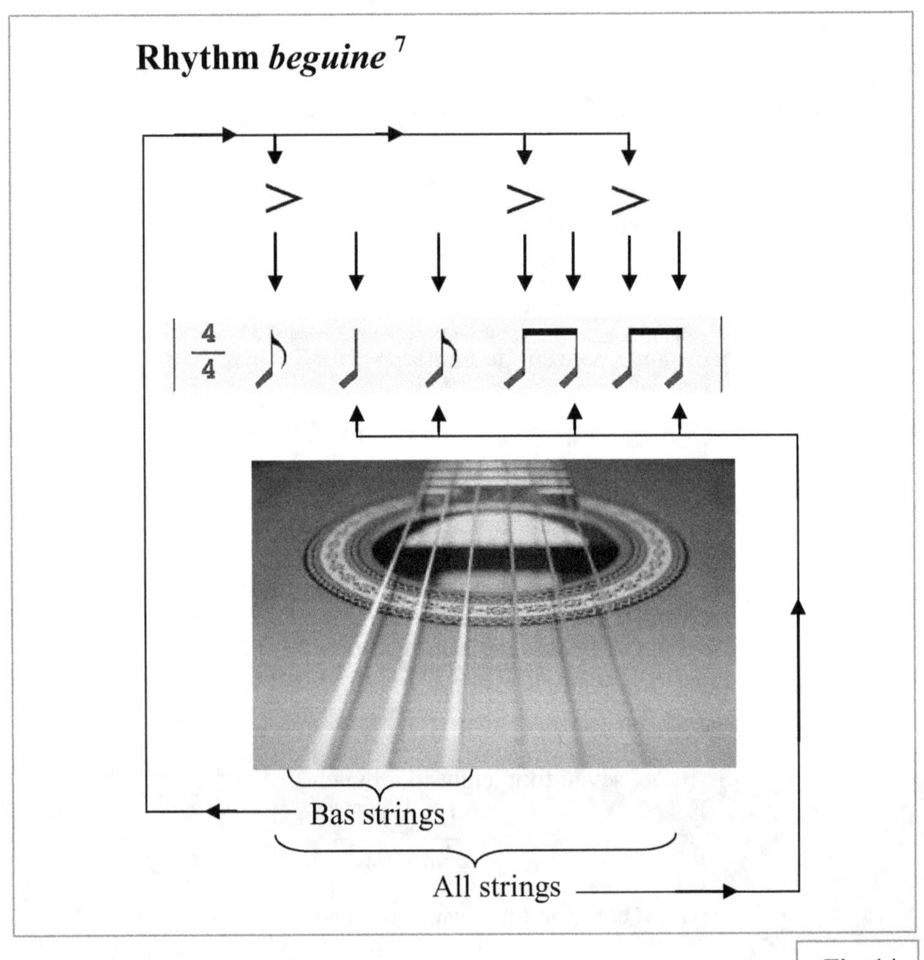

Fig. 14

---

[7] Begine is very popular rhythm; see page 57.

Cuando sali de la Habana valgame dios,

Nadie me ha visto salir si no fui yo.

Y una linda Guachinanga Alla voy yo.

Que se vino tras de mi, que se senor.

Si a tu ventana llega una paloma,

Tratala con carino que es mi persona.

Cuentale tus amores, bien de mi vida,

Coronala de flores que es cosa mia.

Ay chinita que si,

Ay que dame tu amor,

Ay que vente conmingo, chinita,

A dodnde vivo yo.

Combination G-major, C- major, D7

C - major

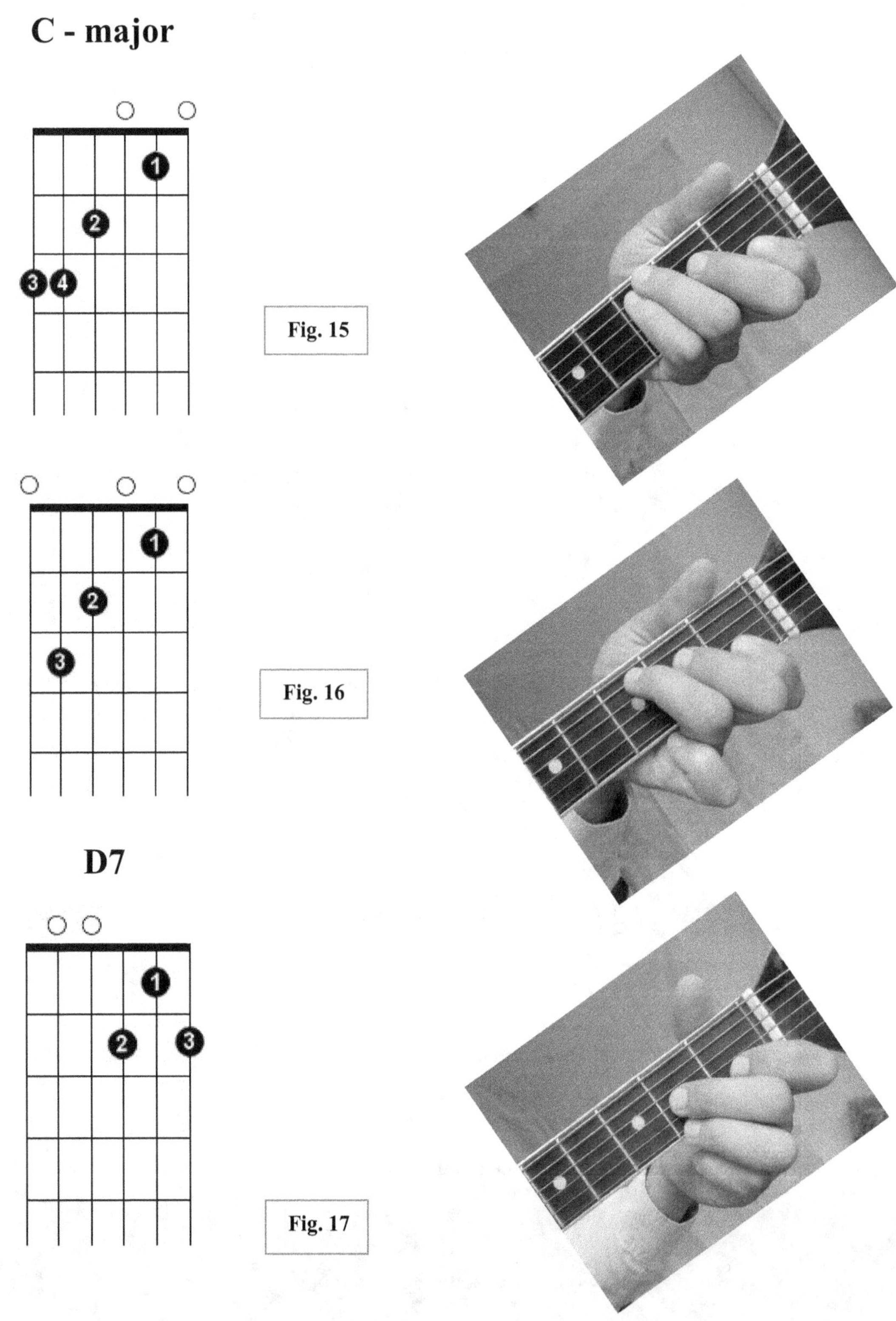

Fig. 15

Fig. 16

D7

Fig. 17

Note:
-   Chord Grip **G-major** is known (see fig. 6).

Example 5:

Jingle bells

> Use the strumming as shown in fig. 8.

Dashing through the snow, in a one-horse open sleigh,

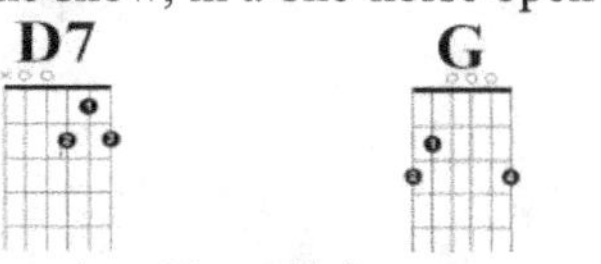

O'er the fields we go, laughing all the way,

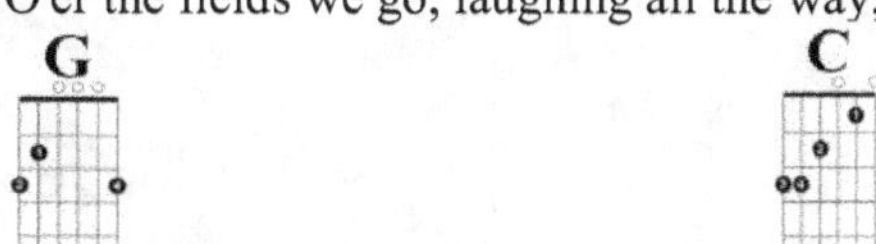

Bells on bobtails ring, making spirits bright,

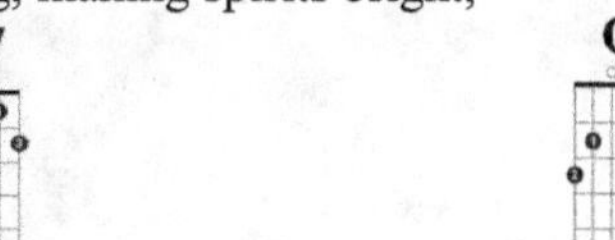

What fun it is to ride and sing a sleighing song tonight, oh

Chorus:

Jingle bells, jingle bells, jingle all the way,

Oh what fun it is to ride in a one-horse open sleigh, hey,

Jingle bells, jingle bells, jingle all the way,

Oh what fun it is to ride in a one-horse open sleigh.

Combinacion C-major, F-major, G7

F - major

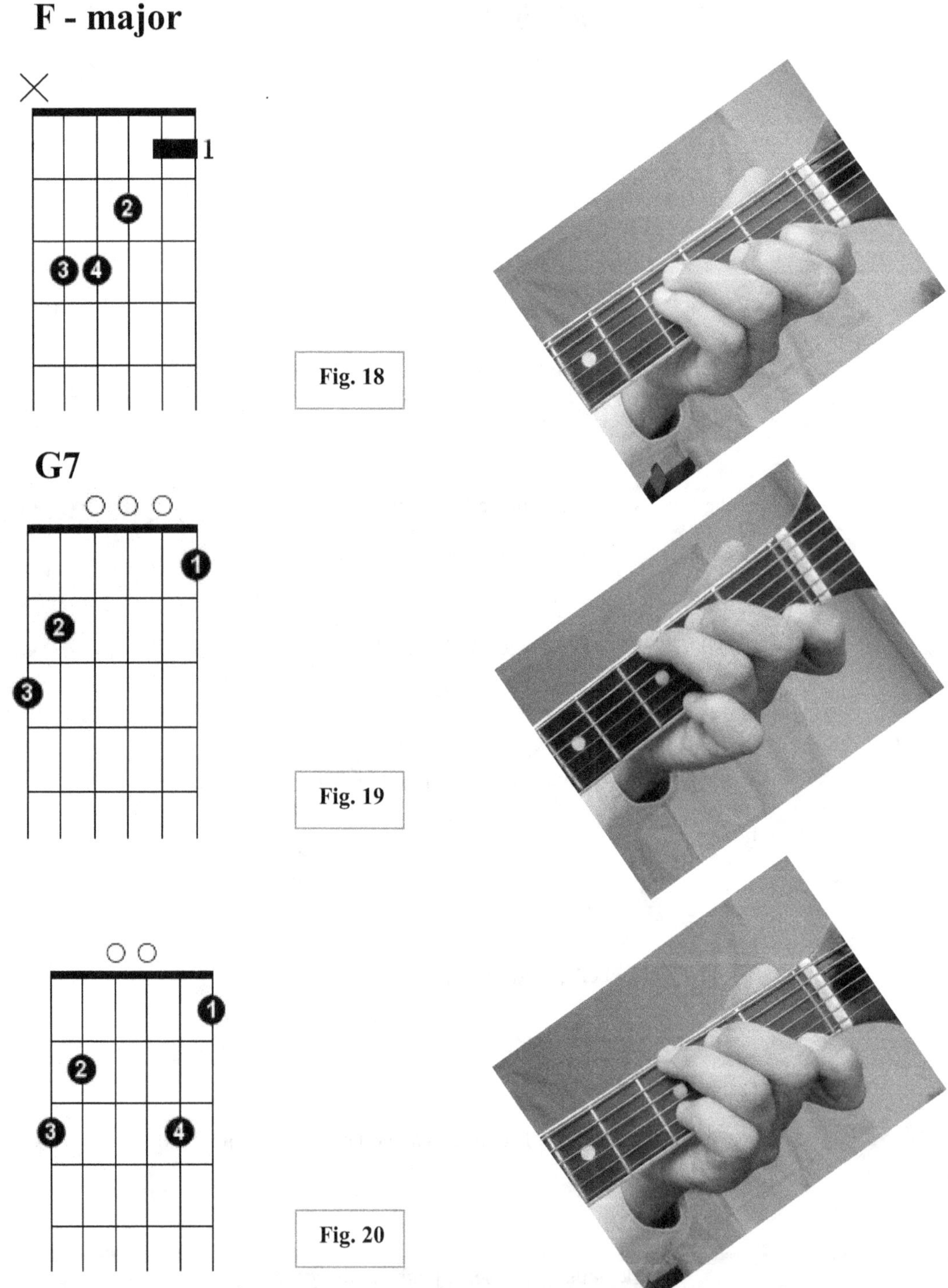

Fig. 18

G7

Fig. 19

Fig. 20

Notes:
- Chord Grip **C-major** is known (see fig. 15 and 16).
- Chord **F-dur** is shown for the reason of methodology and practise (better systematization chord), but it does not belong to the group of *open chords*. This will be discussed later.

Example 5:

Happy birthay to you

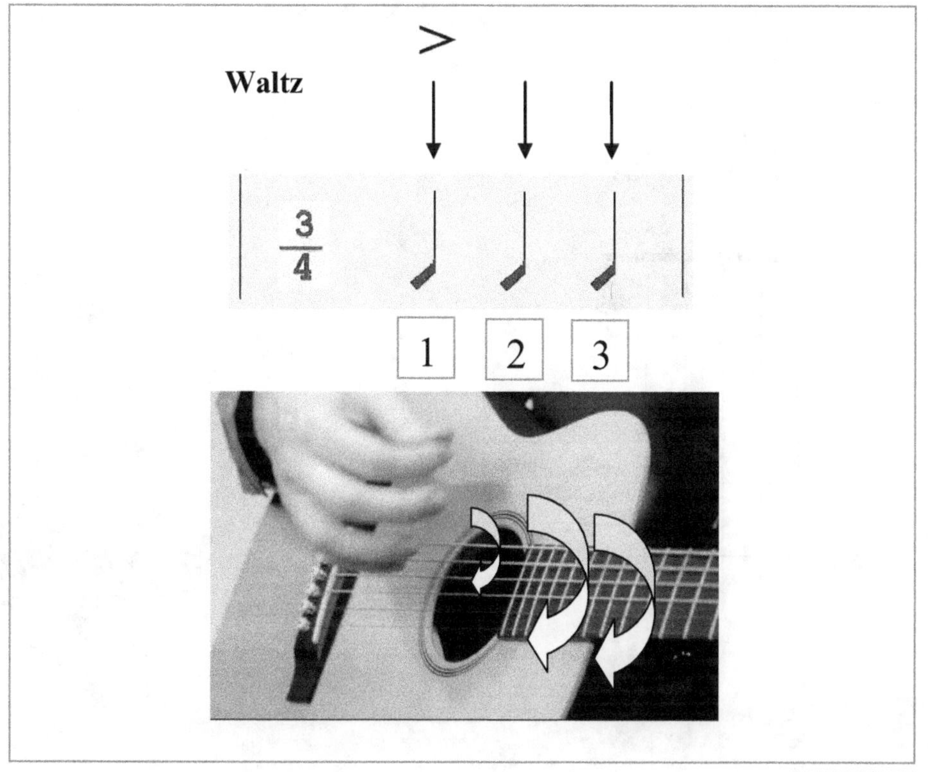

C   G7
Happy birthday to you

C
Happy birthday to you

C7   F
Happy birthday my darling

C   G7   C
Happy birthday to you.

Note:

-   When playing a waltz the first ton is accented and playing on Bass strings.

Combinacion F-major, B^b - major, C7

B^b - major

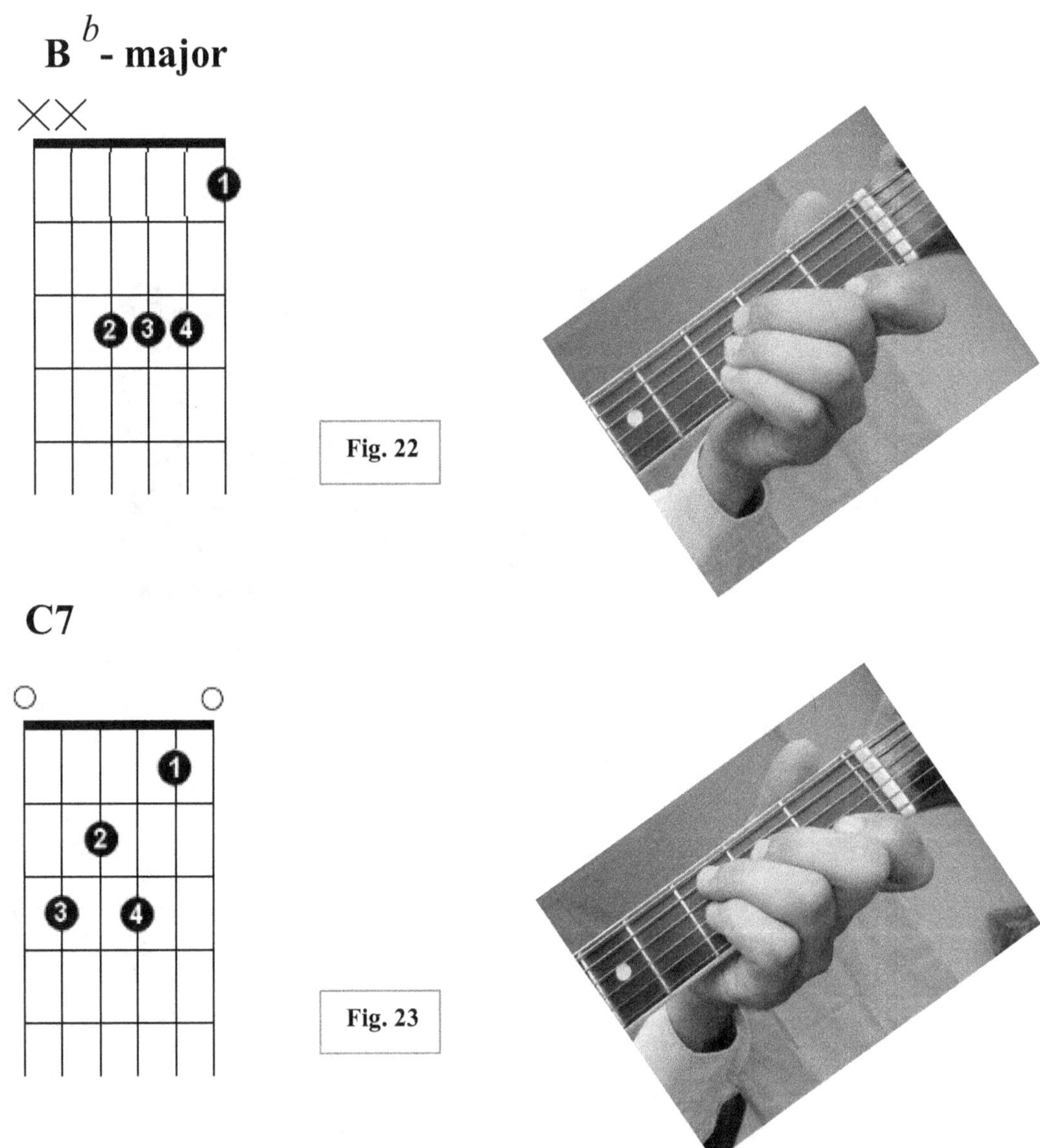

Fig. 22

C7

Fig. 23

Notes:

- Chord Grip **F-major** is known (see fig. 18).
- **B^b-major** also does not belong to the group of *open chords*. The same note applies as the chord **F-major** on page 28th.

Minor chords

A - minor

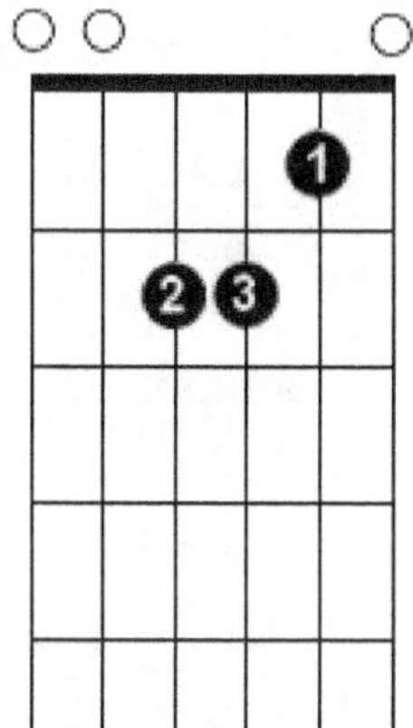

Fig. 24

D - minor

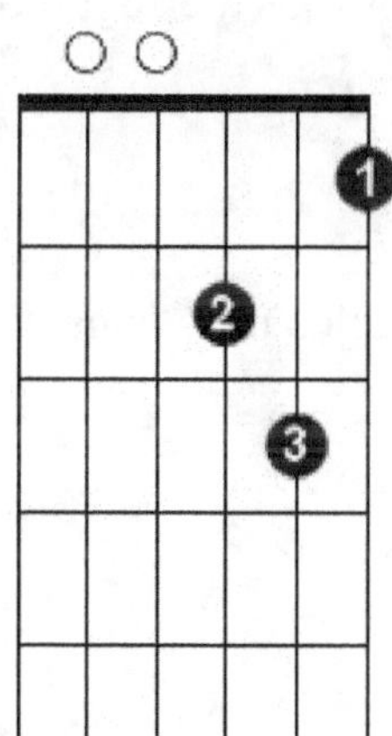

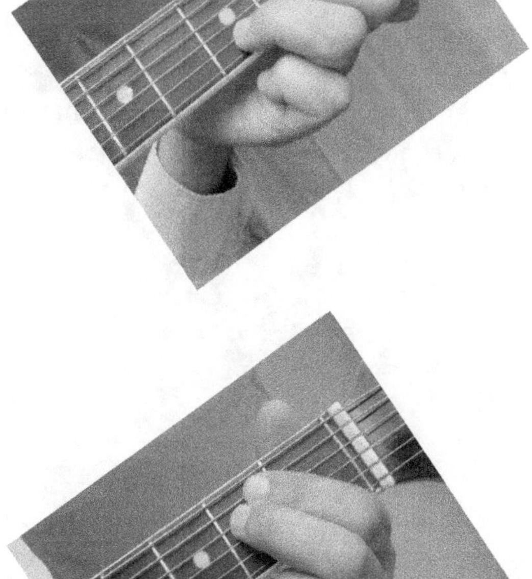

Fig. 25

E-minor

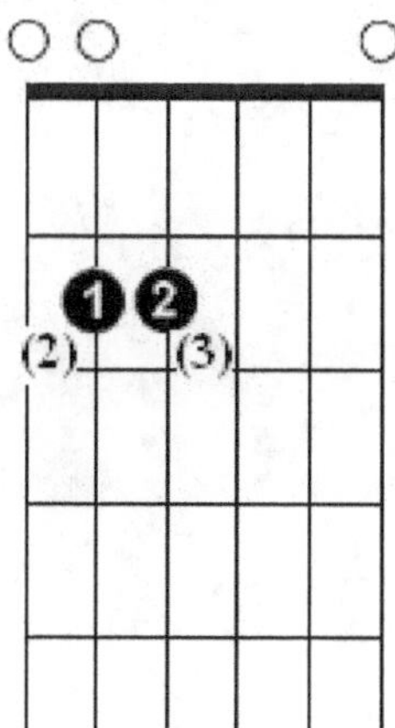

Fig. 26

Example 7:   **Bésame mucho**

Use the strumming as shown in fig. 14 (*beguine*)

Am   Dm   A7   Dm   E7   Am

Bésame, bésame mucho, como si fuera esta noche La última vez,

A7   Dm   Am   F   E7   Am

Bésame, bésame mucho, que tengo miedo a perderte, perderte después

Dm   Am   E7   Am

Quiero tenerte muy cerca mirarme en tus ojos Verte junto a mi

Dm   Am   B7   E7

Piensa que tal vez mañana Yo ya estaré lejos muy lejos de ti.

Bésame, bésame mucho …

Example 8:   **House of the rising sun**

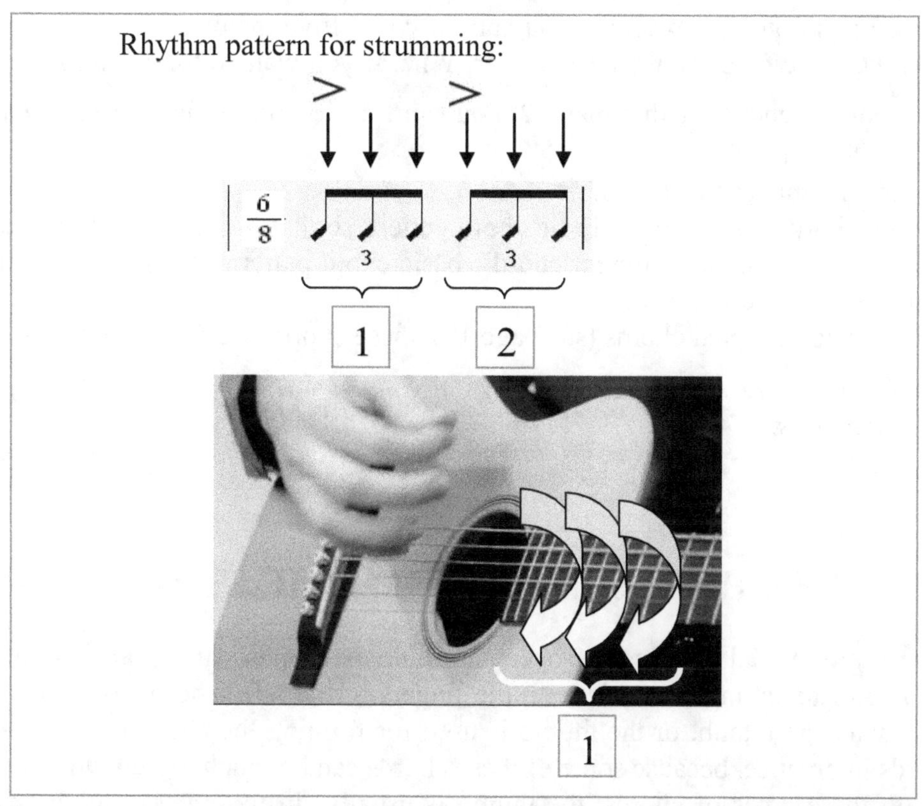

Am   C   D̄   F

There is a house in New Orleans,

Am   C   E7

They call the "Rising Sun",

Am   C   D   F

It's been the ruin of many a poor girl,

Am   E   Am   E7

And God, I know, I'm one.

Verse 2:

My mother was a tailor
She sewed my new blue jeans
My father was a gamblin' man
Down in New Orleans.

MOVEABLE CHORDS

Movable chords [8] can be played anywhere along the fingerboard. You can't play every chord in the guitar's open position. For example, you can only play five major chords in the open position; to remember, these are C, D, E, G and A-major. What if you wanted to play an F or B chord, ar how about an $F^{\#}$ or G^{b} chord for that matter? You can't do it without using a ***movable chord.*** It's the same thing with minor chords.

What are actually moveable chords?

These are the chords that form the basic chord pattern so that it can be easily relocatable across all frets fingerboard, giving the different chords; basic chord patterns can be „carry" up and down the fingerboard to create new chords.

Within the division adopted chords (see page 17), these chords are divided into

- *Movable Chords in which some strings are muted* and
- *Barre chords.*

MOVEABLE CHORDS IN WHICH SOME STRINGS ARE MUTED

These chords are formed by "closing" open chords so that "open" strings are (usually) muted.

Muting some of the strings is made with the fingers of the left hand; usually (but not always) the last strings with the thumb, or the thumb is used for forming the chord grips. Many guitarists use these chords in practice, because some of these chords can be much more favorable than some barre chord. With these types of chords, the thumb is usually in *wrapped* position (see fig 3 on page 16th).

The following are the most typical grips major, minor and dominant 7th chords from this group of chords.

Major chords

F-major

This is the chord we met before (see fig. 18). In that example, the fingers press first five strings in a way that shows the block chord.

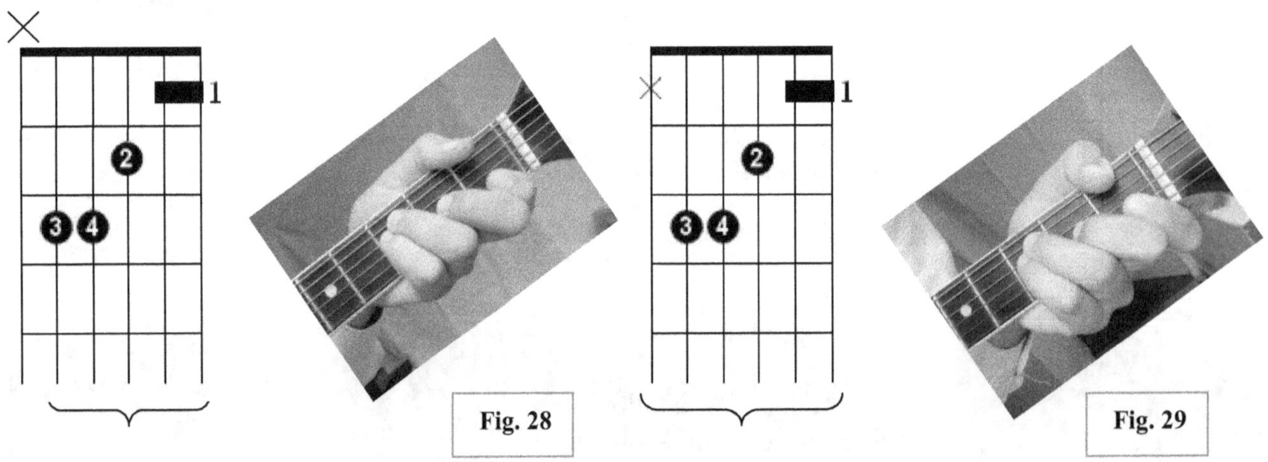

Fig. 28

Fig. 29

---

[8] Every movable chord has the basis of an open chord. **F - major** chord is formed from **E-major** (see fig. 13) so that the grip moves on the next higher fret up and first and second string is pressed with first finger.

The last (sixth) string is not played. However, there are the following two solutions (fig. 27, 28):
1 /slight touch of the sixth string finger to prevent its vibration, and it will not be heard when playing through it; thus allowing playing from all six strings (see fig. 27);
2 / when thumb pressure at the point marked with $\times$, 6th strings participate in the construction of chords, and can be played across all the strings (see fig. 28).

In this case, **F-major** is basic chord pattern. Regardless of which form is applied (fifth or sixth string chord), the basic chord pattern (F-major) can be moved translationally on any fret fingerboard. Depending on what fret the chord grip is set, it will produce a certain chord.
This is best illustrated by the following attachments (fig. 30).

F-major, as a basic chord, on the next higher fret of neck gives $\mathbf{F}^{\#}$**-major** ($\mathbf{G}^{b}$**-major**), and further **G-major**, $\mathbf{G}^{\#}$**-major** ($\mathbf{A}^{b}$**-major**) … etc. The picture also shows three different hand positions on the neck (on the first, fifth and ninth fret), giving the **F-major, A major, $\mathbf{C}^{\#}$-major**.

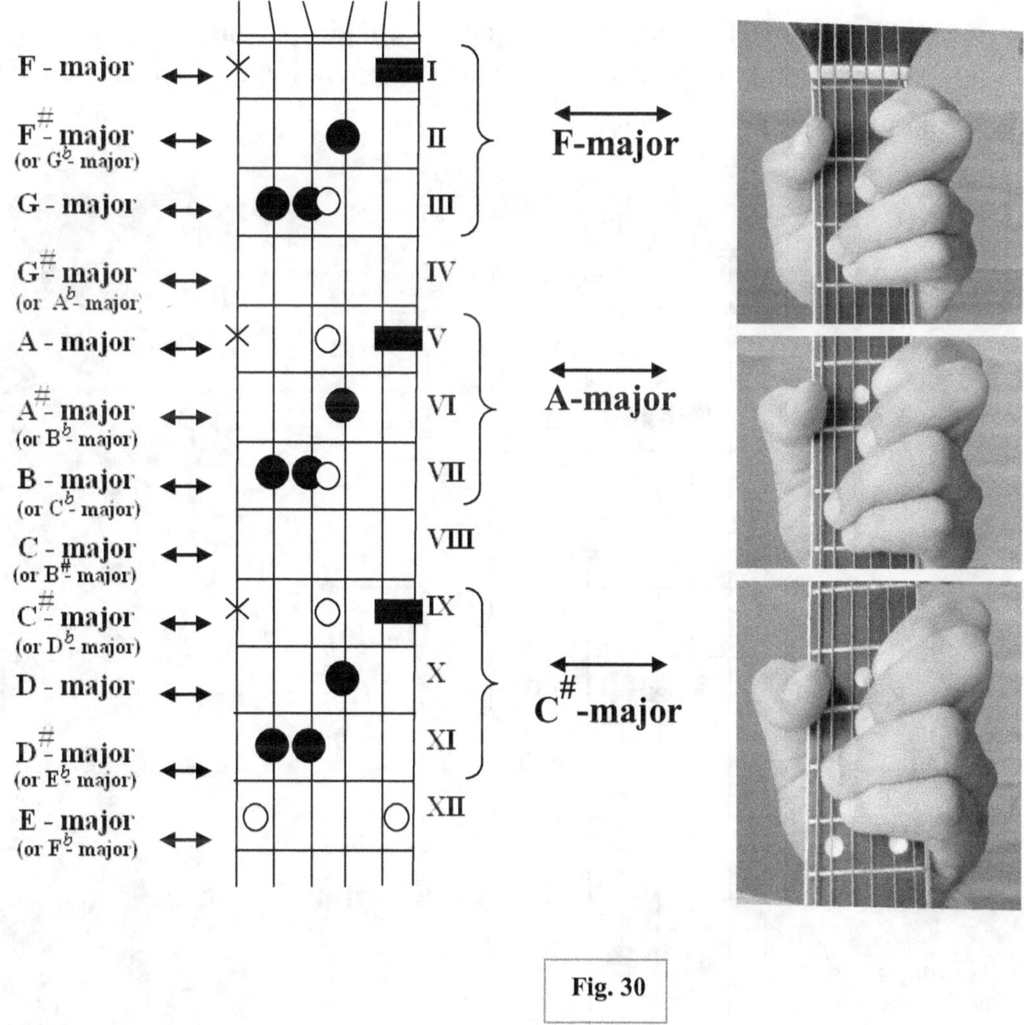

Fig. 30

Note:

  - Play the **A-major** chord with this image and the chord with fig. 9 - it is a variational grips for the same chord.

A$^{\#}$- major (B^{b}-major)

It is the chord that came from A-major as an open chord. This chord can also be play in two ways:
1 / only the first four strings (see fig. 31);
2 / through all the strings, with the last two muted (see fig. 32).

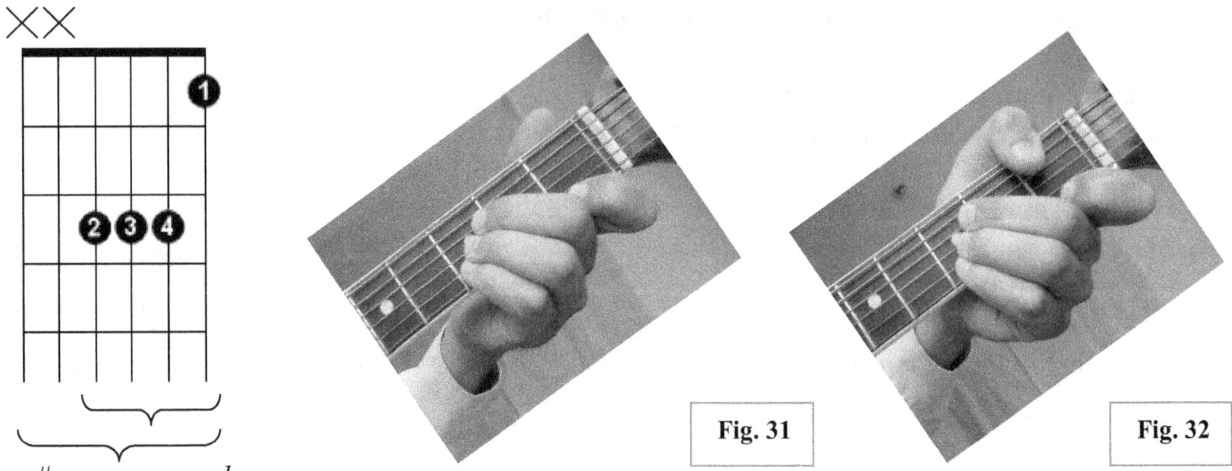

Fig. 31

Fig. 32

A$^{\#}$-**major** (or B^{b}-**major**), as a basic chord, on the next higher fret of neck gives **B-major**, and further **C-major**, **C$^{\#}$-major** (**D^{b}-major**), **D-major**, **D$^{\#}$-major** (**E^{b}-major**), … etc. The picture (fig. 33) also shows three different positions of hand on the neck (on the first, fifth and ninth fret), giving the A$^{\#}$-**major**, **D-major**, F$^{\#}$-**major**.

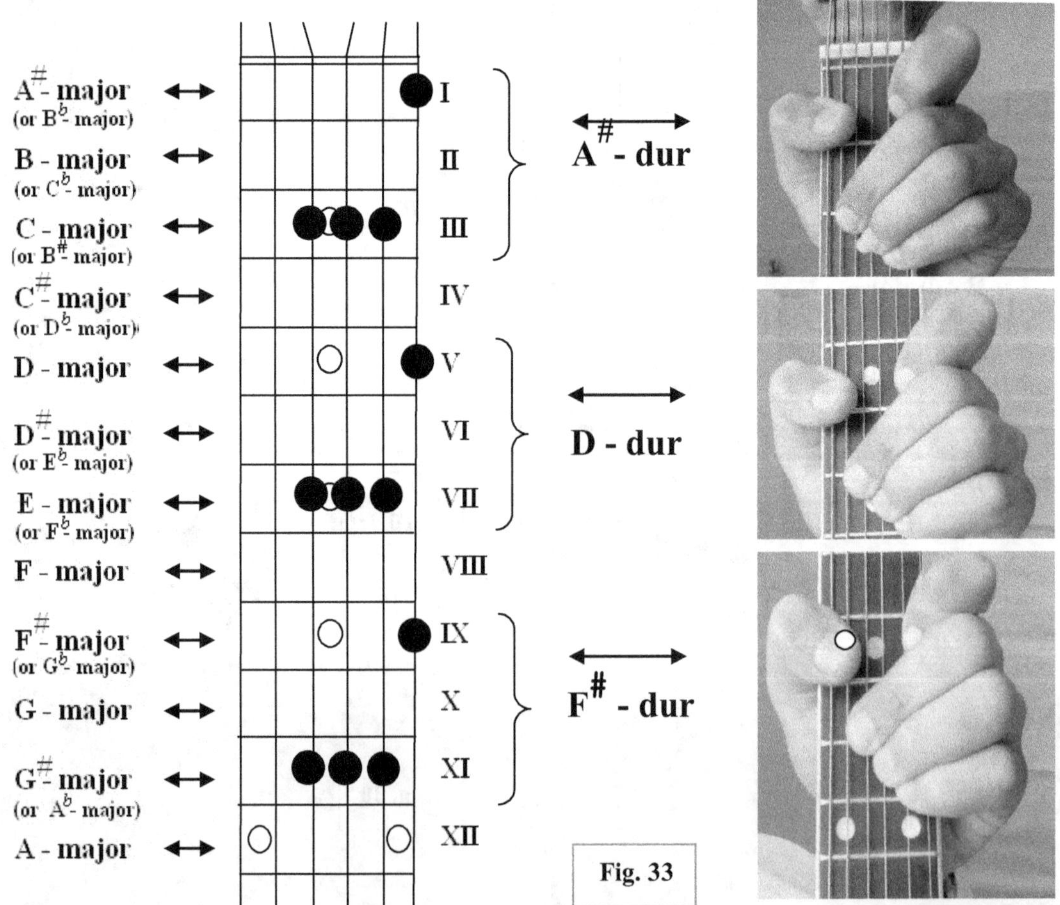

Fig. 33

Note:
- Play the **D-major** chord with this image and the chord with fig. 5 - it is a variational grips for the same chord.

C$^{\#}$-major (D^{b}-major)

In fig. 34 and 35 shows the chord grip **C$^{\#}$-major**. With the same reasoning as for the two previous examples, **C$^{\#}$-major** as a basic chords on the next higher frets of neck gives **D-major**, and further **D$^{\#}$-major** (**E^{b}-major**), **E-major**, … etc.

C$^{\#}$ - major

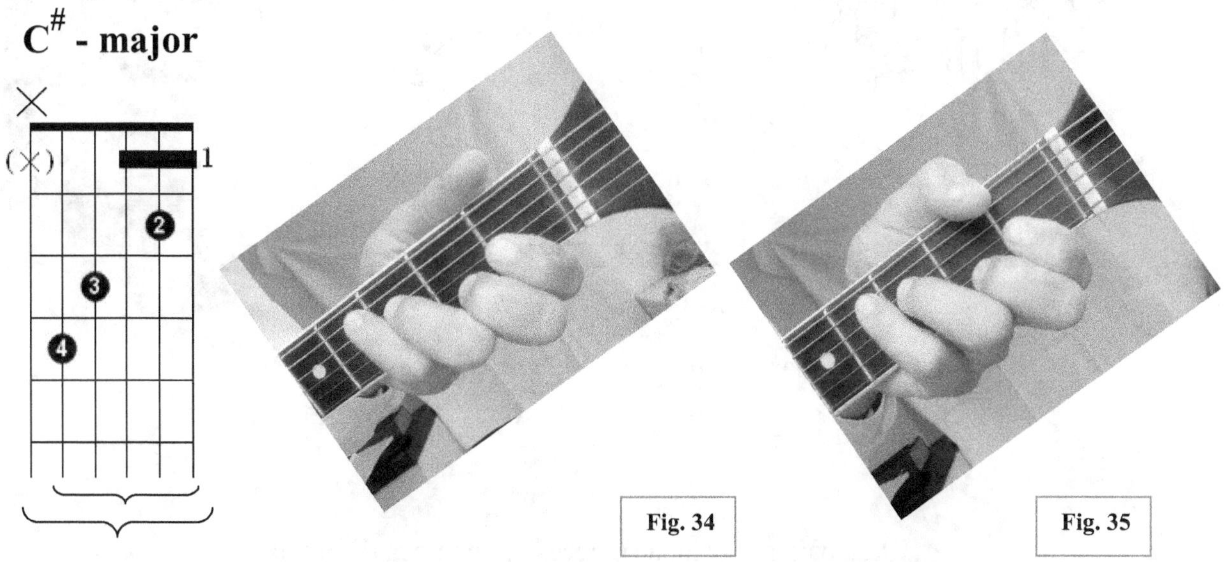

Fig. 34

Fig. 35

Example 9:

La bamba

Fig. 36

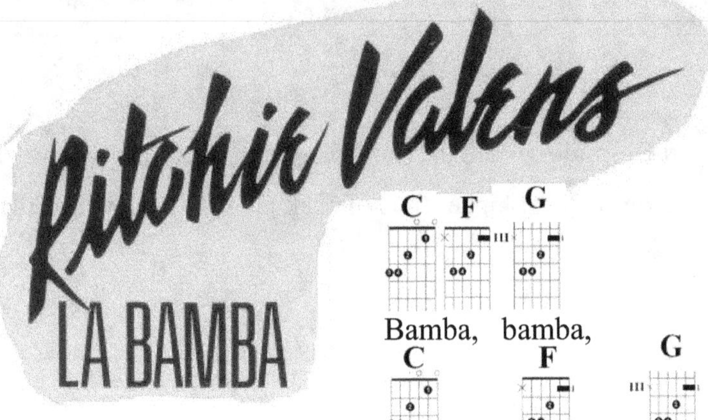

Bamba, bamba,

Bamba, la bamba, la bamba.

Para bailar la bamba,

Para bailar la bamba se necesita una poca de gracia

na poca de gracia pa' mi, pa' ti, ay ariba , ariba

Ay ariba ariba por ti sere, por ti sere, por ti sere.

Yo no soy marinero,

Yo no soy marinero, soy capitan, soy capitan, soy capitan.

Bamba,   bamba,

Bamba, la bamba, la bamba.

Para bailar la bamba …

Minor chords

Without additional comments, here are a few very favorable **minor** chords from this group of *moveable chords*.

F-minor

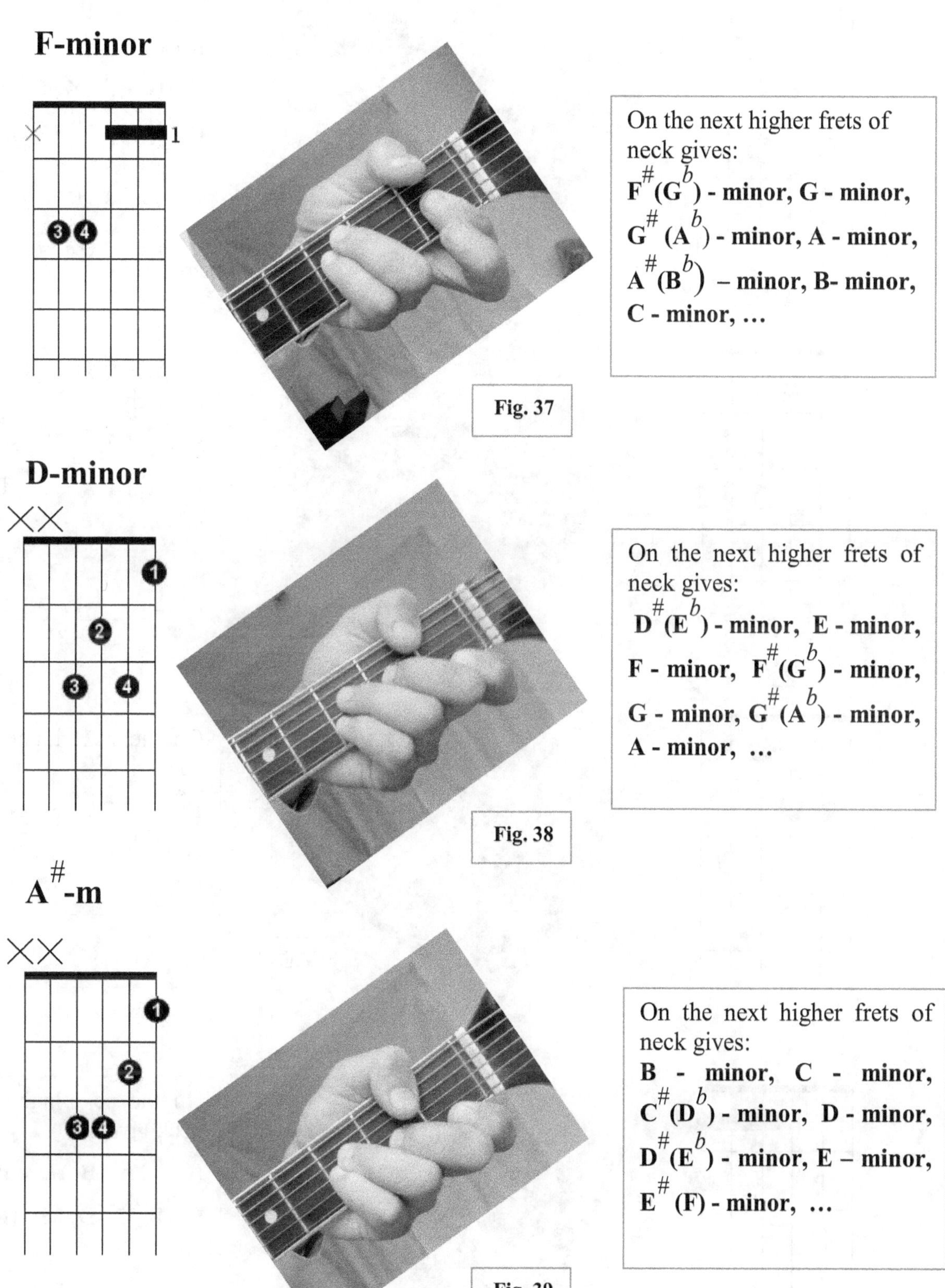

On the next higher frets of neck gives:
$F^{\#}(G^{b})$ - minor, G - minor, $G^{\#}(A^{b})$ - minor, A - minor, $A^{\#}(B^{b})$ – minor, B- minor, C - minor, …

Fig. 37

D-minor

On the next higher frets of neck gives:
$D^{\#}(E^{b})$ - minor, E - minor, F - minor, $F^{\#}(G^{b})$ - minor, G - minor, $G^{\#}(A^{b})$ - minor, A - minor, …

Fig. 38

$A^{\#}$-m

On the next higher frets of neck gives:
B - minor, C - minor, $C^{\#}(D^{b})$ - minor, D - minor, $D^{\#}(E^{b})$ - minor, E – minor, $E^{\#}$ (F) - minor, …

Fig. 39

Dominant 7th chords

The following shows some very favorable grips dominant seventh chords from this group of chords.

C7

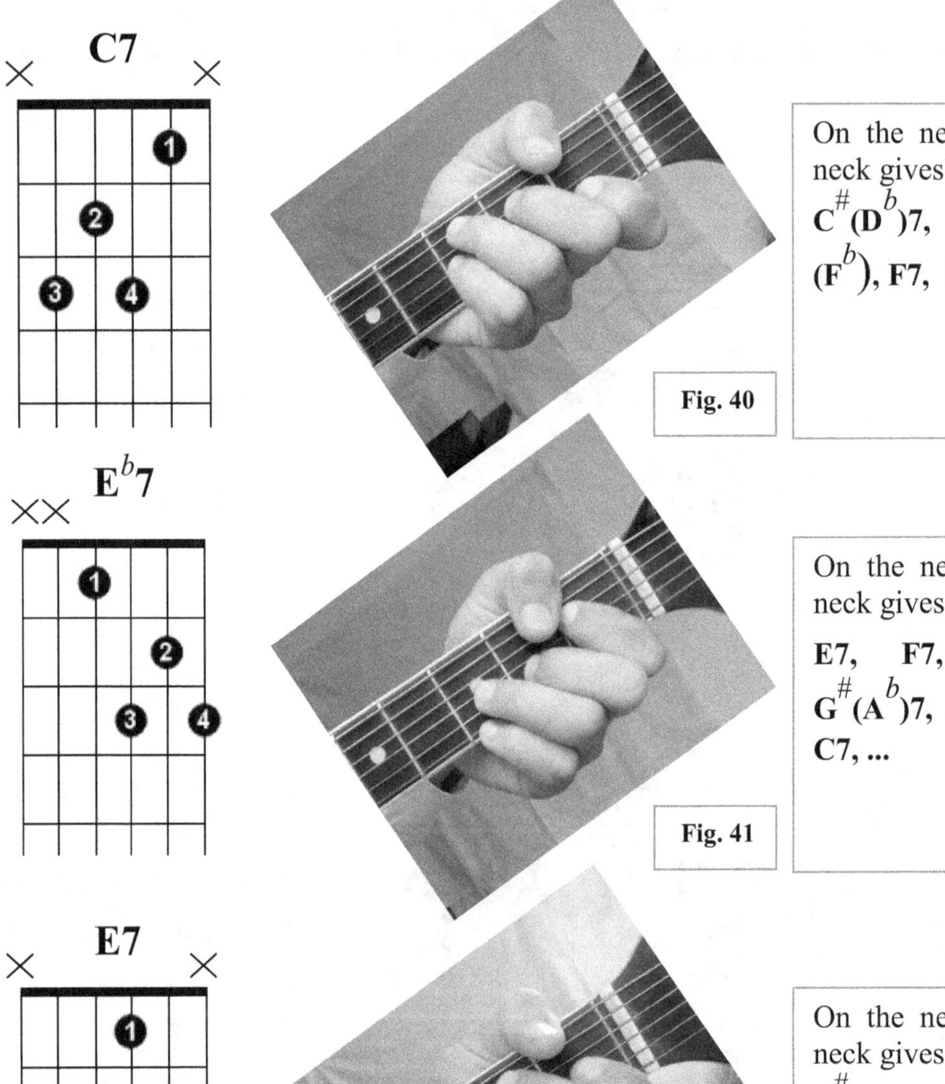

On the next higher frets of neck gives:
$C^{\#}(D^{b})7$, **D7**, $D^{\#}(E^{b})7$, **E7** (F^{b}), **F7**, $F^{\#}(G^{b})7$, **G7**, ...

Fig. 40

$E^{b}7$

On the next higher frets of neck gives:

E7, **F7**, $F^{\#}(G^{b})$, **G7**, $G^{\#}(A^{b})7$, **A7**, $A^{\#}(B^{b})7$, **B7**, **C7**, ...

Fig. 41

E7

On the next higher frets of neck gives:

$E^{\#}7$ **(F7)**, $F^{\#}(G^{b})7$, **G7**, $G^{\#}(A^{b})7$, **A7**, $A^{\#}(B^{b})7$, **B7**, **C7**, ...

Fig. 42

$A^{b}7$

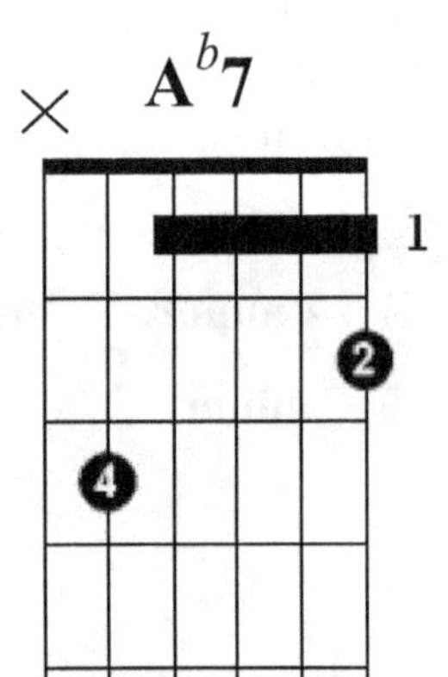

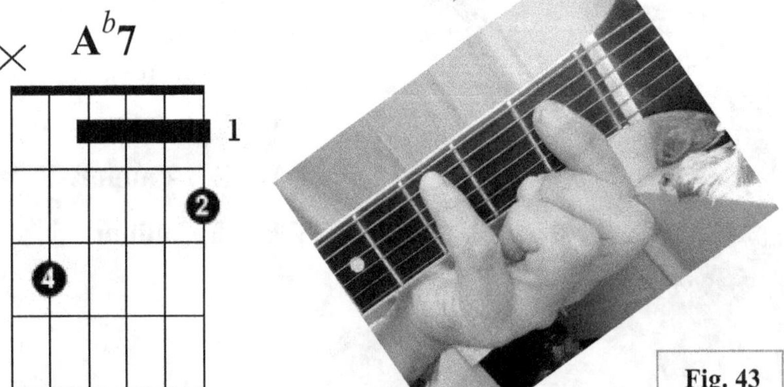

On the next higher frets of neck gives:

A7, $A^{\#}(B^{b})7$, **B7**, **C7**, $C^{\#}(D^{b})7$, **D**, $D^{\#}(E^{b})7$, **E7**, ...

Fig. 43

Note:
- Chord grips C7 and E7 are shown before (Fig. 23 and 10) under the title *open chords*; here the first and the last string are played empty. In this case, the first and the last string on the guitar are muted. The last string is muted using thumb, and the first one using the one that is easiest to touch (almost spontanoulsy).

Example 10:

Sixteen tons

<table><tr><td>Use the strumming as shown in fig. 13.</td></tr></table>

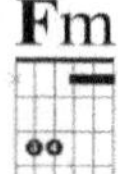

Fm

Some people say a man is made outa mud

A poor man's made outa muscle 'n blood...

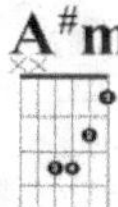

A#m

Muscle an' blood an' skin an' bones

Fm   **C7**   **Fm**

A mind that's weak and a back that's strong.

Verse 2:

You load sixteen tons an' whaddya get?
Another day older an' deeper in debt
Saint Peter doncha call me 'cause I can't go
I owe my soul to the company store.

Example 11:

It's now or never

Use the strumming as shown in fig. 14 *(beguine)*

It's now or never; come hold me tight,

Kiss me my darling; be mine to-night.

To-morrow, will be too late;

It's now or never; my love won't wait.

When I first saw you, with your smile so tender,

My heart was captured, my soul sur-rendered.

I'd spend a lifetime, waiting for the right time,

Now that you're near; the time is here at last.

It's now or never …

Verse 2:

Just like a willow, we would cry an ocean,
If we lost true love, and sweet de-votion.
Your lips ex-cite me; let your arms in-vite me,
For who knows when, we'll meet a-gain this way?

BARRE CHORDS

Barre chords are also a movable chords. It is obvious that they also originate from the open chords. For barre chord is characteristic that the index finger of the left hand pressures (like a tape) several strings or all the strings in a particular fret of fingerboard. When the index finger pressures only a few strings - three or four, then it is a small barre; when the index finger pressure all six strings, then it is a great barre.

Barre chords are very present in practice, they affect the proper guitar holding and the correct position of the left hand.

Which one will be used in practice, barre chords or chords in which some strings are muted, is the sole guitarist's decision.

The following are the most typical grips major, minor and 7 chords from the group barr chords.

Major chords

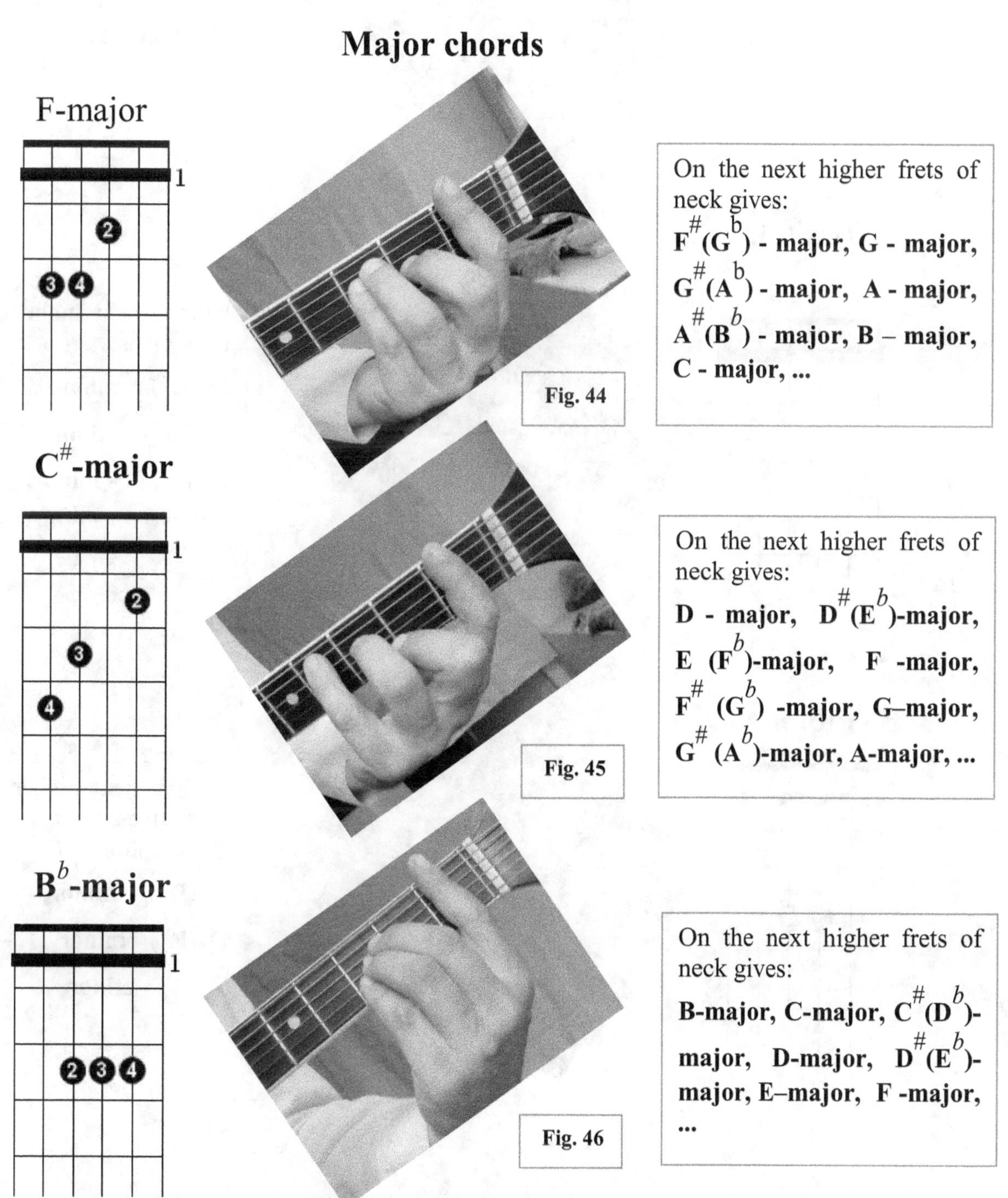

F-major

$C^{\#}$-major

B^{b}-major

On the next higher frets of neck gives:
$F^{\#}(G^{b})$ - major, G - major, $G^{\#}(A^{b})$ - major, A - major, $A^{\#}(B^{b})$ - major, B – major, C - major, ...

On the next higher frets of neck gives:
D - major, $D^{\#}(E^{b})$-major, E (F^{b})-major,   F -major, $F^{\#}(G^{b})$ -major, G–major, $G^{\#}(A^{b})$-major, A-major, ...

On the next higher frets of neck gives:
B-major, C-major, $C^{\#}(D^{b})$-major, D-major, $D^{\#}(E^{b})$-major, E-major, F -major, ...

Minor chords

F-minor

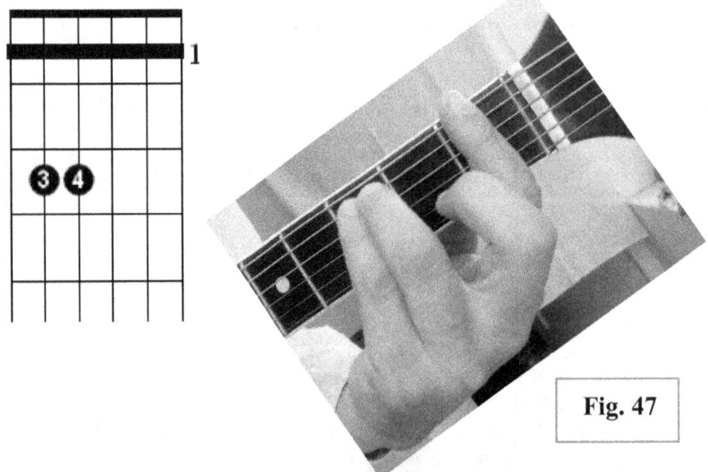

Fig. 47

On the next higher frets of neck gives:
$F^\#(G^b)$ - minor, G -minor, $G^\#(A^b)$ - minor, A - minor, $A^\#(B^b)$ - minor, B – minor, C - minor, ...

D-minor

Fig. 48

On the next higher frets of neck gives:
$D^\#(E^b)$ - minor, E - minor, $E^\#(F)$ - minor, $F^\#(G^b)$ - minor, G - minor, $G^\#(A^b)$ - minor, A - minor, ...

B^b-minor

Fig. 49

On the next higher frets of neck gives:
B - minor, C - minor, $C^\#(D^b)$ - minor, D-minor, $D^\#(E^b)$ - minor, E – minor, $E^\#(F)$ - minor, ...

Dominant chords

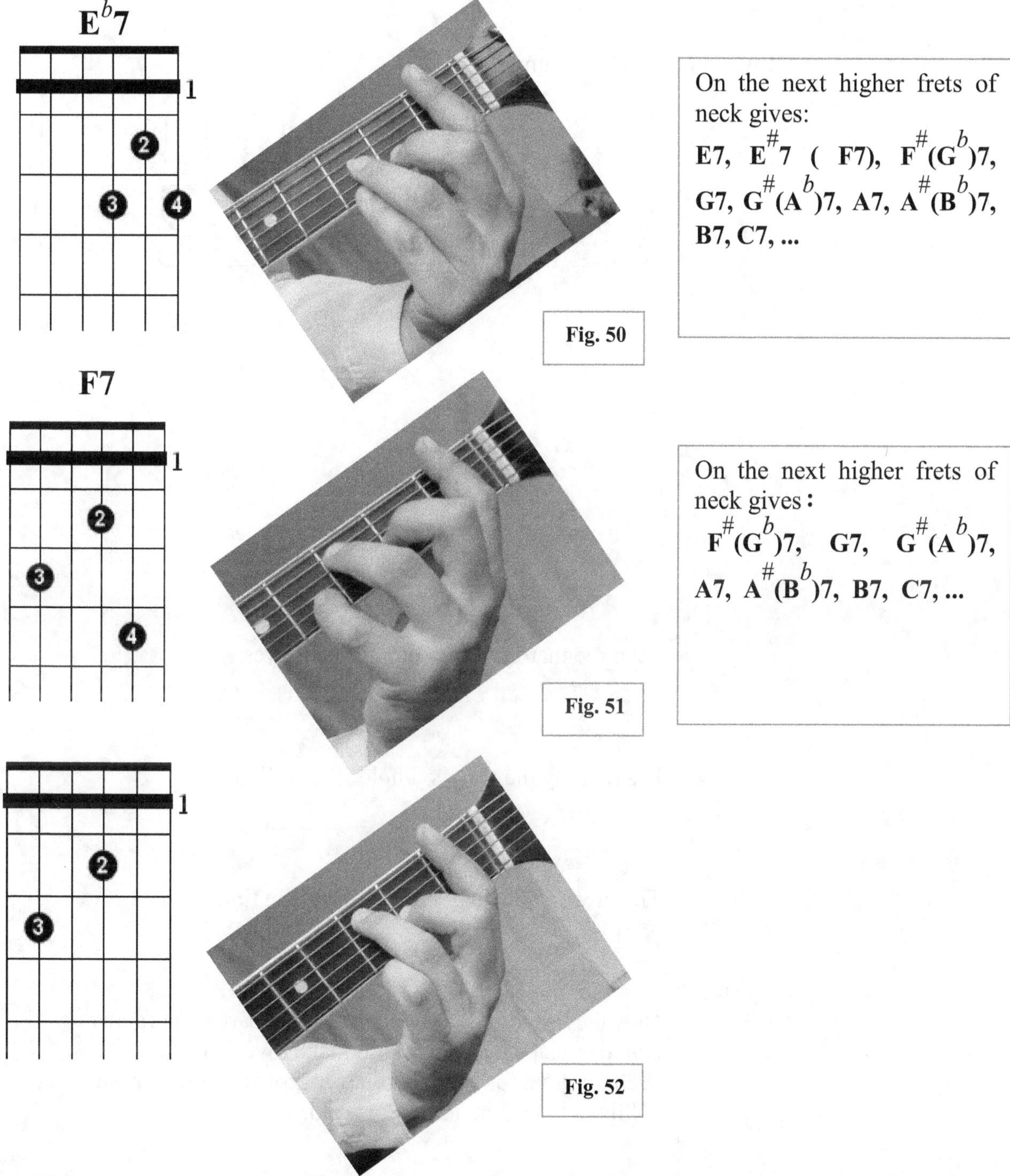

E^{b}7

Fig. 50

On the next higher frets of neck gives:
E7, E$^{\#}$7 (F7), F$^{\#}$(G^{b})7, G7, G$^{\#}$(A^{b})7, A7, A$^{\#}$(B^{b})7, B7, C7, ...

F7

Fig. 51

On the next higher frets of neck gives :
F$^{\#}$(G^{b})7, G7, G$^{\#}$(A^{b})7, A7, A$^{\#}$(B^{b})7, B7, C7, ...

Fig. 52

Note:
-    The last two chord grips are alternatives to chord F7.

Example 12:

Crying time

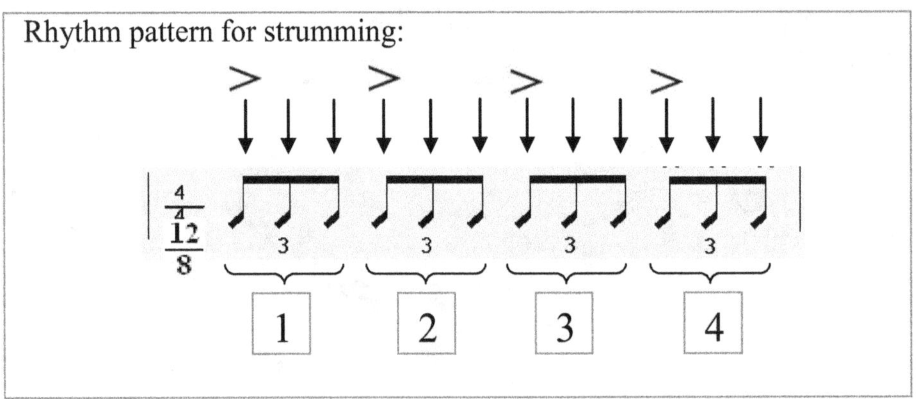

G   **D7**

Oh, it's crying time again, you're gonna leave me.

G

I can see that far away look, in your eyes.

G7   **C** **Cm**

I can tell by the way you hold me, darling.

G   **D7**   **G**

That it won't be long, before it's crying time.

Verse 2:

      Now they say that absence makes the heart grow fonder
      And that tears are only rain to make love grow
      Well my love for you could never grow no stronger (stronger)
      If I lived to be a hundred years old.

Example 13:

Massachusetts

> Use the strumming as shown in fig. 13.

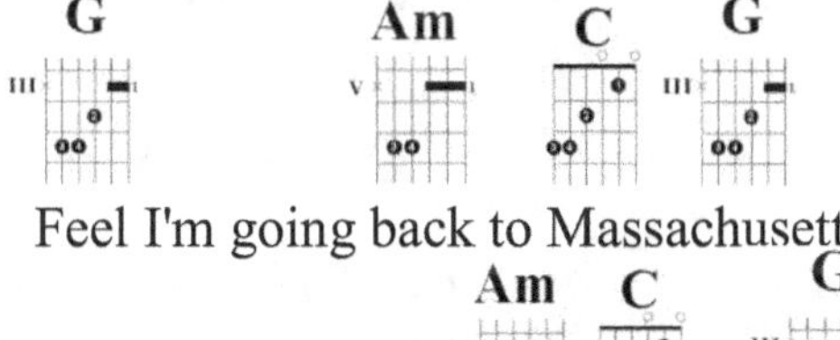

Feel I'm going back to Massachusetts

Something's telling me I must go home

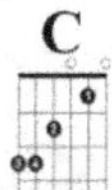

And the lights all went out in Massachusetts

The day I left her standing on her own.

Verse 2:

Try to hitch a ride to San Francisco
Gotta do the things I wanna do,
And the lights all went out in Massachusetts
They brought me back to see my way with you.

Example 14:

Blue Spanish Eyes

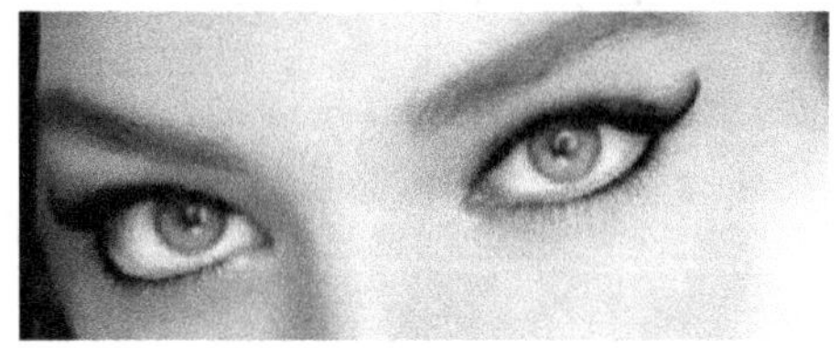

Rhythm *beguine*; see fig.14

G   **D7**

Blue Spanish Eyes, teardrops are falling from your Spanish Eyes,

G

Please, Please don't cry, this is just adios and not goodbye,

G7   **C**

Soon I'll return, bringing you all the love your heart can hold,

Cm   **G**   **D7**   **G**

Please, say si, si, say you and your Spanish Eyes will wait for me.

Verse 2:

Blue Spanish Eyes, Prettiest eyes in old Mexico,
True Spanish Eyes, please smile for me once more before I go,
Soon I'll return, bringing you all the love your heart can hold,
Please, say si, si, say you and your Spanish Eyes will wait for me.
Say you and your Spanish Eyes will wait for me.

Example 15:

Lara's song (dr Zhivago)

Use the strumming as shown in fig. 21 (waltz)

G   **D7**

Somewhere, my love, there will be songs to sing,
G

although the snow covers the hope of spring.
D7

Somewhere a hill blossoms in green and gold.
G

and there are dreams, all that your heart can hold.

C   **G**

Someday we'll meet again, my love,
B^b **F**   **B**^{b} **D7**

someday whenever the spring breaks through.

Verse 2:

You'll come to me out of the long ago
Warm as the wind, soft as the kiss of snow
Till then my sweet
Think of me now and then
God speed my love till you are mine again.

ADVANCED CHORDS

Chords which are described in this chapter are used in melodies that have a bit more complex harmony. In doing so, I singled out only those chords, which are most present in practice, in no particular order and classification. Also, I did not go into theoretical explanations relating to these chords.

Chords in this chapter are described in the following order: Augmented chords (aug, +), major sixth (6), minor sixth (m6), Major Seventh (maj7), minor seventh (m7), diminished (dim) and Ninth Chords (9).

Augmented triad chords

They are marked in the following ways: aug, +, 5+, +5, $^{\#}$.

This chord is a chord of tones that at the same time it contains. Since it contains three tons, the title bears the name of three chords.

Image shows version chord grip that is at the same time **A+**, **C$^{\#}$+** and **E$^{\#}$+**:

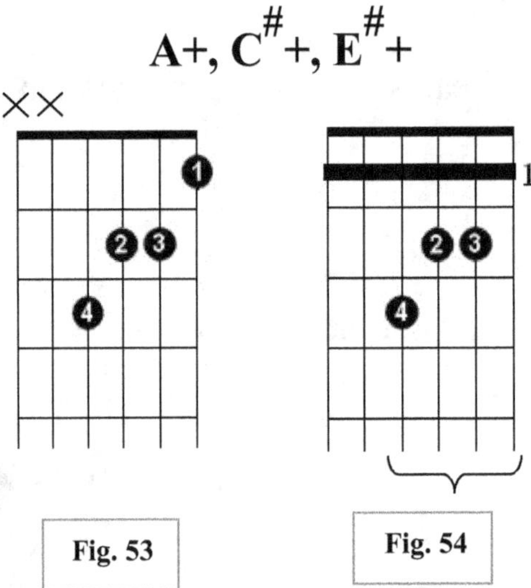

Displayed are two versions of the same chord grips. In the second case (fig. 54) is barre chord - index finger across all six strings (because it is so favorable), although the chord is played only the first four strings.

Major 6th chords

They are marked in the following ways: **6, maj6, M6**.

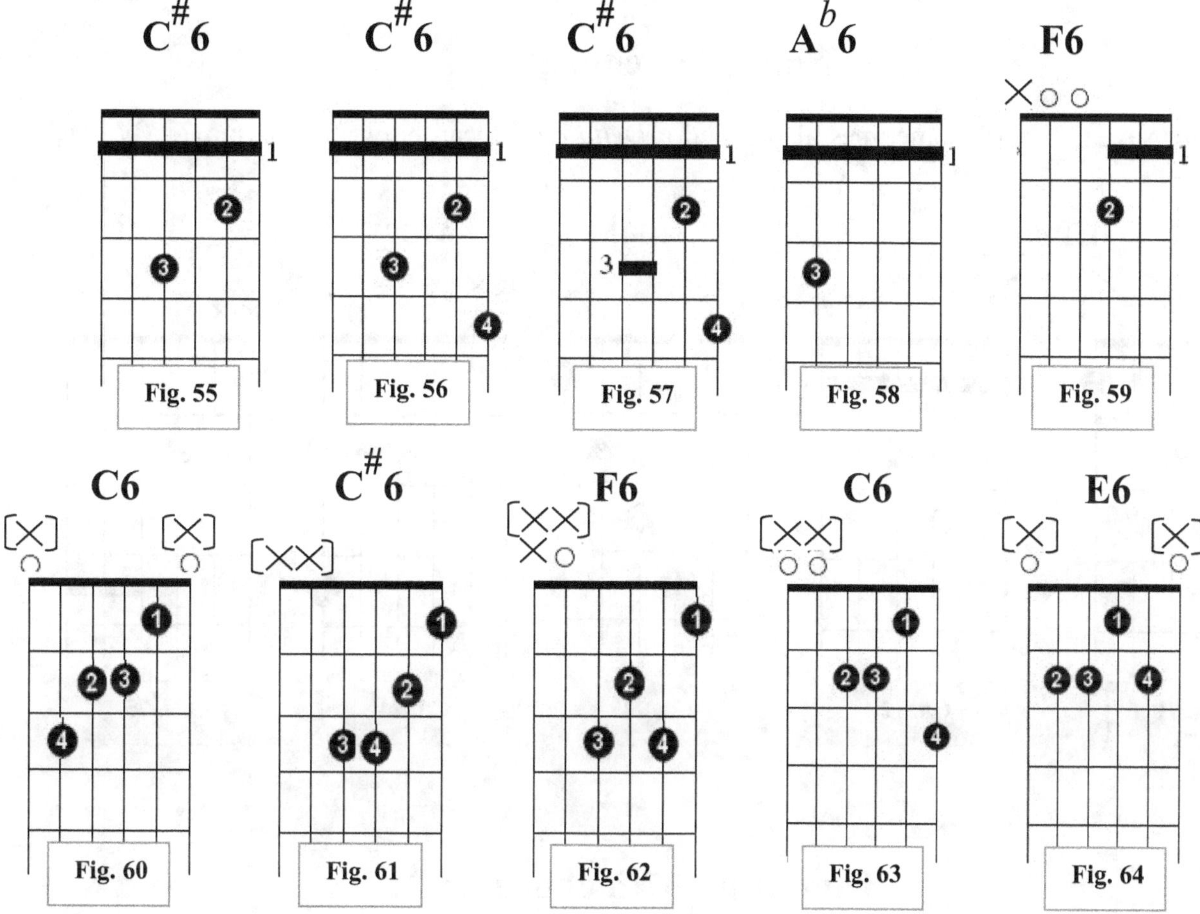

Note:
- Chords in the second row are *open chords*, but can easily be converted into the *moving chords* (by muting individual strings) and are used in all the areas of fingerboard,. As such, they are very convenient to use.

Minor 6th chords

They are marked **m6,** for example **Cm6**.

Note:
- All shown *open chord* grips are very applicable in practice and they can be used to form *moveable chords*. For chord grips in the pictures and ... just play the first four strings (because it is so favorable), even though the chord grips are shown as a large barre (across all six strings).

Major 7th chords

The major seventh chord, sometimes also called a *Delta chord*, can be written as **maj7, M7, 7+,** Δ7, Δ.

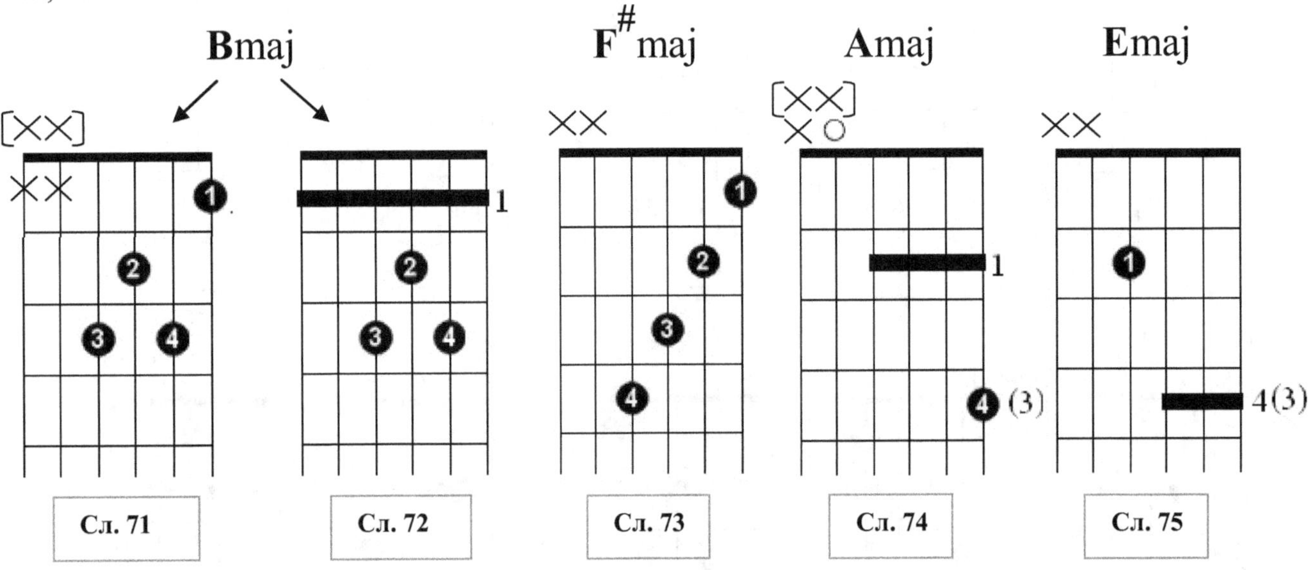

Diminished 7th chords

They are marked in the following ways: **dim7, um,** $^{\circ}$.

As plus chord, this chord is a chord of all tones at the same time it contains. Since it contains four tons, the title bears the name of four chords. For example, shown in pictures chord grips 76 and 77 (both chord grips refers to the same chord), which represents a chord that is at the same time Ddim7, Fdim7, A^{b}dim, C^{b}D.

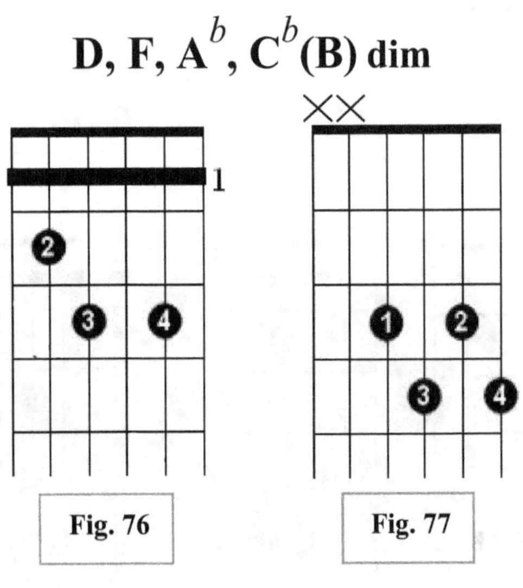

On the next higher frets of neck gives the following chords: **Cdim7, E^{b}dim7, G^{b}dim7, A^{b}dim7,** moving to a third field **C$^{#}$dim7, Edim7, Gdim7, A$^{#}$dim7,...** etc.

Minor 7th chords

They are marked in the following ways: **m7, min7, -7**

These chords are already known. How? Without theoretical explanation, we will give the following rule: Minor 7th chords contain the same tones (only in a different order of tones) as the corresponding major 6th chords. The relationship is as follows (see attached table).

What does this mean in practice? Chord grips with the left and right are identical.

As the chord grips of major sixth chords are already known (see page 51), these are also the chord grips of minor 7th chords.

Minor sixth chords	Corresponding Minor seventh chords
C6	Am7
D6	Bm7
E6	$C^{\#}$m7
F6	Dm7
G6	Em7
A6	$F^{\#}$m7
B6	$G^{\#}$m7

Dominant 9th chords

They are marked in the following ways: **9, 7/9, dom9**

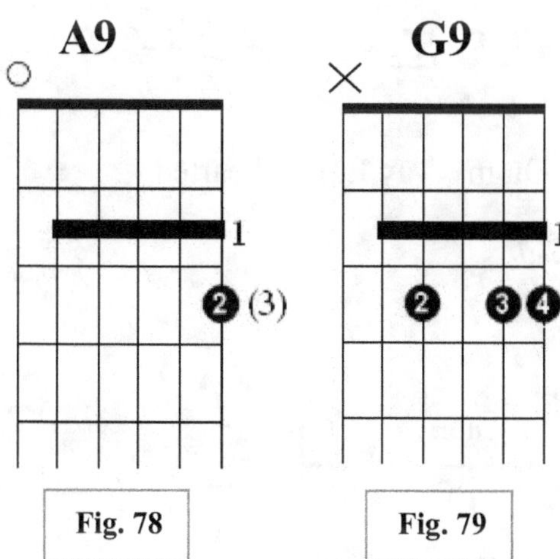

Fig. 78   Fig. 79

Damping guitar strings

Damping (also referred to as choking) is halting the vibration of the strings using the left hand.

It is a technique where, shortly after playing the strings, the sound is reduced by relaxing the left hand fingers' pressure on the strings (left hand damping or left-hand muting).

It is demonstrated in the attached video.

Example 16:

Fascination

> **Slow Waltz**

C   **G+** **Cmaj7**

It was fascination I know

C   **Cdim**   **Dm** **A7**

And it might have ended Right then, at the start

Dm   **Dm7** **Dm6**

Just a passing glance Just a brief romance

Dm   **Fm**   **Dm7** **G7**

And I might have gone On my way Empty hearted

C   **G+** **Cmaj7**

It was fascination I know

C   **Cdim**   **Dm** **A7**

Seeing you alone With the moonlight above

Dm   **F**   **Dm7** **G7**

Then I touch your hand And next moment I kiss you

Dm7   **G7** **C**

Fascination turned to love.

Example 17:

Strangers in the night[9]

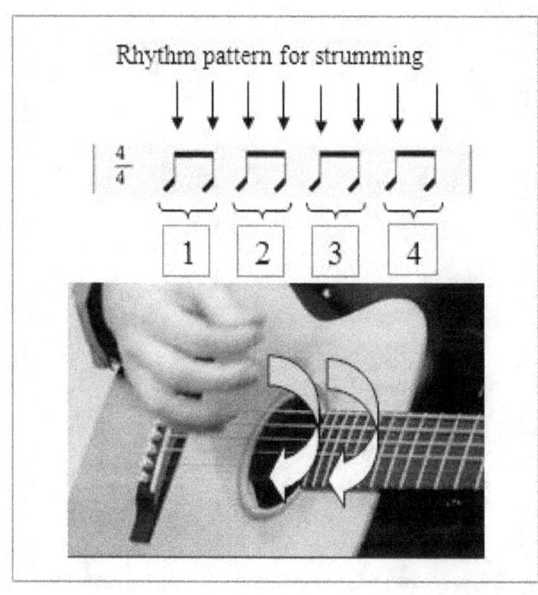

Сл. 80

F

Strangers in the night exchanging glances,

Fmaj7

Wondering in the night what were the chances,

F6   **Gm**

We'd be sharing love before the night was through,

Gm

Something in your eyes was so inviting,

Gm7

Something in your smile was so exciting,

Gm6   **C7**   **F**

Something in my heart told me I must have you.

Cm7

Strangers in the night, two lonely people,

D7

We were strangers in the night up to the moment,

Gm   **Gm7**

when we said our first hello, little did we know,

F   **Dm**

Love was just a glance away.

Gm   **C7**

A warm embracing dance away - and

F

Ever since that night we've been together,

Fmaj7

Lovers at first sight in love forever,

C7   **F**

It turned out so right for strangers in the night.

---

[9] There are differences in the harmony of this song. This is the version that I used.

Example 18:

My Way

Use the strumming as shown in fig. 8

Verse 2:

Regrets, I've had a few, but then again, too few to mention.
I did what I had to do and saw it through without exemption,
I planned each charted course, each careful step along the byway,
And more, much more than this,
I did it my way.

III. RHYTHM GUITAR IN THE ORCHESTRA

Rhythm guitar in the previous section refers only to a case when the accompaniment by guitarist is realized independently. Certain differences exist when it comes to rhythm guitar in an orchestra, and it is reflected in the following:

Depending of the rhythm of the melody, rhythm guitar in the orchestra must be in collision with the bass option (contrabass or bass guitar), and using down and up strokes in the precise way through strings, so that the tonal and rhythmic corresponds with the bass option.

Here's how it would look at the case of several well-known rhythms. Previously, we will adopt the Convention which refers to the down and up strokes. Namely, in the previous examples were used rhythmic patterns for the right hand using arrows. In the following we will use the way which is used within the rhythm - guitar, respectively:

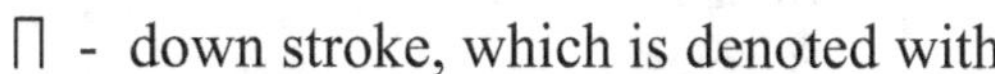

∏ - down stroke, which is denoted with ↓

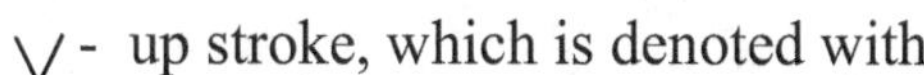

∨ - up stroke, which is denoted with ↑

2/4 Tact:

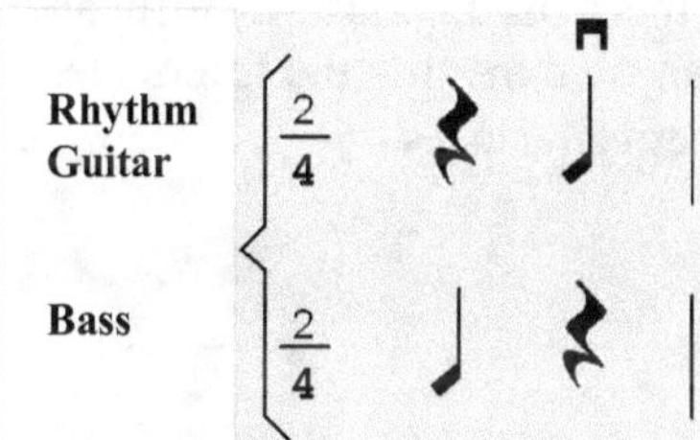

2/4 Tact, with some differences in accent, is very common in many musical genres (polka, czardas, country music, swing ...).
The first stroke (the first quarter note) realized on bass guitar, and it's accented tone, and the other (second quarter) belongs to the rhythm guitar and it's melodic part, which is realized by down stroke through all guitar strings.

¾ Tact:

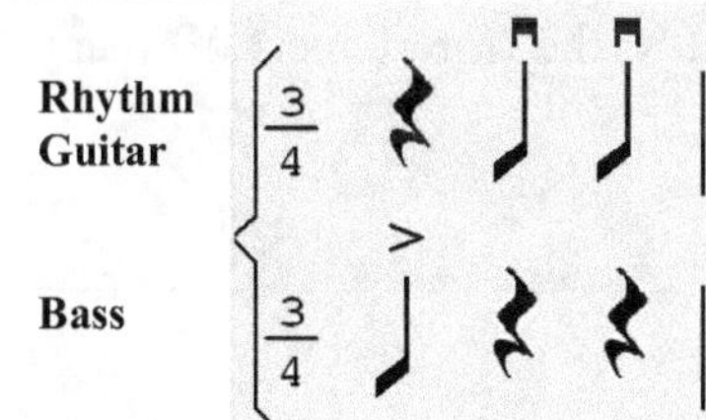

¾ Takt is the best known as the waltz. The first - accented stroke (the first quarter note) is realized on bass guitar, and the second two strokes (the second and third quarter) are melodic parts that is realized by two down strokes through all guitar strings.

Beguine:

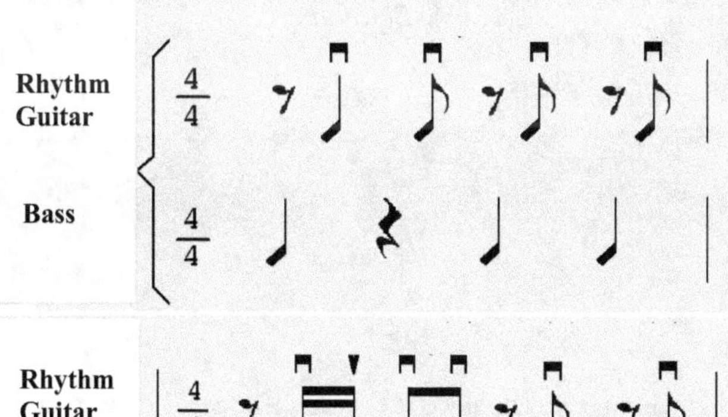

Originating from the Caribbean. *beguine* is attractive and very well-known rhythm in the world. In the orchestra is realized in a way that rhythm guitar responds to the bass strokes which are played in the first, third and fourth quarter within the tact.
A bit more attractive version of the beguine is shown in the second example.

9/8 Tact[10]:

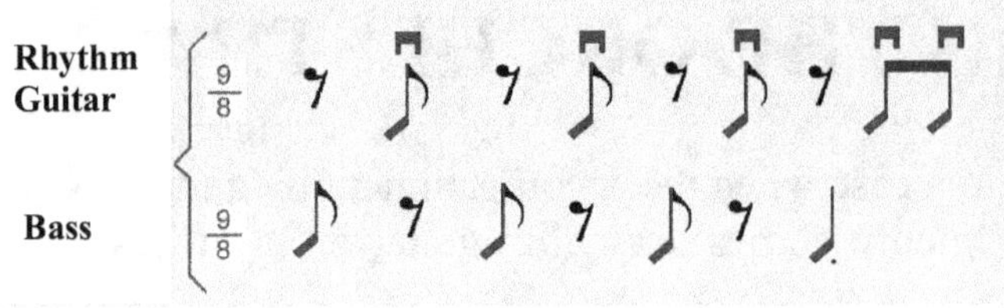

9/8 Tact is one of the most popular rhythm from the group of odd rhythmes and is very frequent in some folk melodies (Macedonia, Bulgaria, Albania).
The first, third, fifth and seventh eighths notes are accented and are played on the bass. Rhythm guitar is playing melodic part in the presented rhythmic pattern.

Tango[11]:

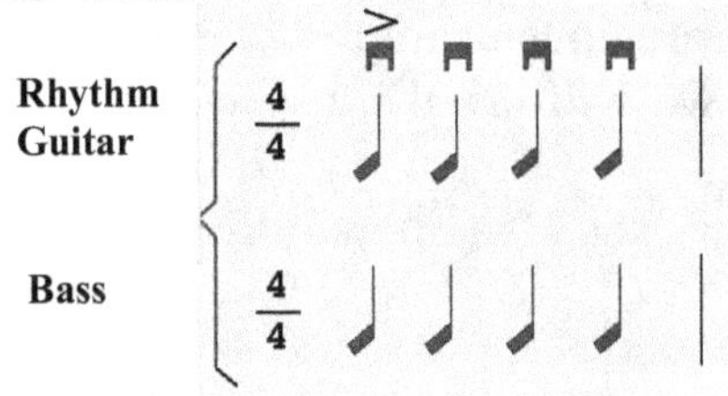

These examples present three versions of the most famous tango - argentine tango.

Rumba:

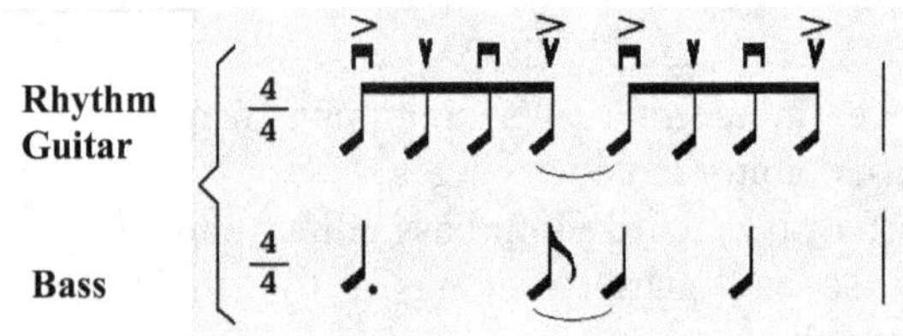

Rumba is one of the most famous Afro-Cuban and Latin American rhythms. It's the forerunner of many Latin American dances.

Samba:

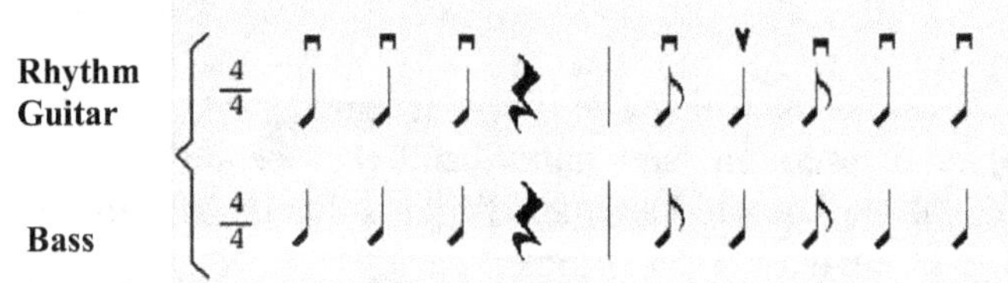

Samba is one of the most famous music and dance rhythms. It's the forerunner of many similar rhythms.

Calypso:

The famous rhythm from Trinidad. Calypso became very famous with *Harry Belafonte.*

---

[10] In this case, it shows the most typical arrangement of eighths within 9/8 tact, since it can be different. I other odd rhythms are pretty represented in some folk melodies, especially 7/8, rarely 5/8 and 11/8, even more rarely 13/8. With different combinations of accented and unaccented eighths within the tact, in the Bulgarian folklore there's tact 27/8.

[11] There are several versions of tango (Spanish, Argentine, Uruguayan, Latin America, ...), as well as various versions of Argentine tango. In this example are shown the most tipicall versions of the Argentine tango.

Literature

Petrovic, Milan Bata, S*kola popularne gitare*, Nota, Knjazevac, III izdanje, 2007.

Petrovic, Milan Bata, S*kola popularne gitare 2 – gitarski ritmovi*, Udruzenje srpskih izdavaca, Beograd, I izdanje, 2013.